THE ADVENTURES OF BARRY O AND TAILGUNNER JOE

Barack Obama and Joe Biden know they have to fix a lot of things. Now, if they could just figure out what those things are.

by

AUSTIN SPEED

For my wife, our son, our dog, our next door neighbors, and all the people who've been suffering through the worst presidency in American history.

"***The Adventures of Barry O and Tailgunner Joe***" is a work of satirical fiction. Any resemblance to real persons living or dead is pretty much intentional.

Copyright © 2012 by Austin Speed

Cover art and interior art by Austin Speed

Chapter One

AND SO IT BEGINS

"Politics is the art of looking for trouble, finding it whether it exists or not, diagnosing it incorrectly, and applying the wrong remedy."

- Ernest Ben

Barack Obama, David Axelrod, and Bill Daley were in the White House Oval Office discussing fundraising strategy for the upcoming campaign. They were using a highly sophisticated code system that the group had developed in case they were overheard. Obama wanted to be able to plausibly deny participating in any illegal campaign activity or campaign fundraising while on government property.

"How's *Operation Crushpublican* going?" Obama asked.

"Well, Mr. President, the *harvest* is slow coming in this year," David Axelrod said.

"Are you telling me that we're behind on *bringing in the corn*?"

"Yes, sir," Axelrod said. "By about forty percent."

"Okay. Let's get the *crop bundlers* to step it up. Don't forget, we need a billion *ears* by next September."

"Well, sir," Bill Daley added, "the *harvesters* we have are very busy and working hard, but we have fewer of them than we did last time."

"Hmmm," Obama said while rubbing his forehead. "What do we have to do to get more people for the *harvest*?"

"Well, sir," Axelrod replied, "it would help to kill more high profile terrorists, like Bin Laden."

"And frankly sir," Daley added, "we don't have any more Bin Ladens or Qaddafis. All the rest of them have names that don't stick. The American people only knew Bin Laden and Qaddafi. They're gone now and the bounce we got from those wins has already receded."

Just then a loud racket erupted down the hall that sounded like large caliber gunfire.

"Wham, ba-bam, ba-bam, ba-bam!!!"

"What the hell is that?" Obama blurted.

Two Secret Service agents pulled their weapons and headed down the hall to confront the situation. Obama followed several steps behind figuring it was safer to be close to the agents than stay behind in the office.

"Wham, ba-bam!!!"

Obama's blackberry buzzed and he saw that it was Michelle. He decided to answer it.

"Whatthehellsgoingondowntheregetcontrolofthesituationthatswaytooloudandlcan'tconcentrateonmywebsite..."

"We're getting it under control, hon," Obama said into the phone.

"Wham, ba-bam, ba-bam!!!"

The agents opened the door of the office where the noise was coming from.

"Hands up!!!! Hands up!!!"

Obama looked in and saw Joe Biden with a couple of Special Forces soldiers. They were dressed in desert camouflage uniforms wearing Kevlar vests, helmets, and sidearms. Biden had his hands on the trigger housing of a belted fifty caliber machine gun set up behind some sandbags. The gun's barrel was pointed out an open office window.

"Wow, did you see that one? He had no idea where to go," Biden said. "Just running back and forth like that. That was funny."

"Hands up!!!" the agents repeated.

Biden looked around and saw the Secret Service agents with their guns drawn. "Okay guys," Biden said. "Let's stop for now."

Obama saw that Joe was also wearing a vest and a helmet along with a set of military goggles.

"Joe, Joe! What are you guys doing?"

"Oh, hello, Mr. President. I thought you were up at Camp David today. Right now we're firing over their heads, Mr. President. Keeping their heads down."

"Keeping whose heads down?"

"The Republicans, Mr. President. After those last midterms we need to do something," Biden said.

"True," Obama said, "but you can't shoot at them, Joe."

"Oh, I'm just firing over their heads, sir. The shots are just warnings."

"Well, Michelle called and says your gun is too loud."

"We're almost done, Mr. President. They've pretty well scattered for now. Besides, I figured this would stimulate things a bit, seeing as how the Stimulus Package was such a dud."

"Well, could you please stop firing?" Obama asked. "You might hit a tourist."

"Okay, sir. I'll stop. But, I was told there are no more tourists in D.C." Biden said, "because of the Stimulus Package and the economy and all."

"Joe, I'm not sure I want to know this actually, but how do you know you're only shooting at Republicans?"

"I have a spotter, Mr. President."

"A spotter? Looking for what?"

"Well, sir, our spotter is looking for those flag lapel pins that the Republicans wear. We've only been shooting at those."

"You're saying that only Republicans wear those pins?" Obama asked.

"To the best of my knowledge, Mr. President," Biden said.

"Well, come on down to the Oval Office with me," Obama said. "I need to talk to you."

"Yes, sir. What's up?" Biden asked as he took off his helmet and vest. The two of them walked toward the Oval Office while talking.

"A reporter's calling in about our tax plan, Joe."

"Our tax plan, sir?" Biden asked. "Hmmm…that's kind of old stuff. We haven't talked about that for a while. Let's give him the stuff from our website."

"We tried that, Joe. He says that's a lot of hooey. If we don't explain it better he's going to take us on," Obama said. "He says he can expose a lot of 'logical holes.' We don't need another distraction from the press right now."

"I'll talk to him, Mr. President," Biden said. "I'll tell him to call Wolf Blitzer. Wolf can explain it. He's good at explaining stuff. I love the way Wolf talks about Cheney."

"That's a good idea, Joe," Obama said as they entered

the Oval Office. "I want to talk to Wolf first." Obama pushed his intercom button, "Put a call into Wolf Blitzer, please."

"YSSSTTT, MMMMMM PSSSSSDDDDD," the intercom replied.

Obama looked at Biden, Daley, and Axelrod. "What did she say?"

"Mmmmmrrrr Prrrrrrrdddt,Wooool Bzzzzzzz, ahhhhh pnnnnn," the intercom crackled.

Axelrod said, "Mr. President, she said that Wolf Blitzer is on the phone, I think."

Obama hit the button to put Blitzer on speakerphone. "Wolf, this is Barack. How's it going?"

"Great, Mr. President. It's good to hear from you. When can we get an exclusive?"

"Soon. Soon, Wolf. Say, I've got you on speakerphone here with Vice President Biden, David Axelrod, and Bill Daley. We have a question for you. We're trying to get a gauge on how our tax plan came across during the campaign. Could you describe my tax plan to me as you understand it?"

"You want me to describe your tax plan to you?" Blitzer asked.

"Yes, Wolf," Obama said, "as you understand it. We're trying to see if we have been clear. We want to take the initiative on tax policy to set things up for 2012."

"Well, Mr. President, as you know you agreed with the Republicans to extend the Bush tax rates until 2012."

"The Bush tax rates? Oh, you mean his tax cuts. Well, that's true but that's temporary," Obama said. "I'm going to be implementing my own tax plan after that. Do you remember what we told people my tax plan was?"

"Well, Mr. President," Blitzer said, "you said, as I recall, you'd be raising taxes on anyone making over 250 thousand. As of the last speech Joe made where he talked about it, before the new agreement, your administration was recommending a tax hike on everybody who makes over 150 thousand. Somebody else, I think it was David Axelrod, said 120 thousand. That's what I recall at any rate."

"That's just about what I was thinking," Obama said. "Thanks, Wolf."

"Goodbye, Mr. President."

Obama disconnected the phone call.

"By the way, Mr. President," Biden said, "I was talking to Barney Frank and he says we have to cut defense by another twenty five percent."

"Did Barney say how we were supposed to do that, Joe?" Obama asked.

"Well," Biden said, "he says we need more friends so we don't have to prepare to fight everybody. He says that you promised that once you were elected and Bush and Cheney were out, the world would be safer."

"Joe, next time you talk to Barney make sure he knows I'm working on that."

"I will, Mr. President. He also says we need to get our friends to line up faster. And, they have to have their own armies and stuff otherwise they don't do us any good as friends."

Bill Daley said, "We could probably recruit a lot of Young Republicans, Mr. President. We send 'em overseas to defend us and some other countries. They love the idea of defending America and our friends."

"That's true, Bill," Obama said.

"One of the things that's really good about this idea," Daley said, "is that when those people are overseas they vote absentee. Their votes won't be counted. They won't get here fast enough."

"How's that, Bill?" Obama asked.

"We used to do it in Illinois all the time. Nobody wanted the military absentee ballots to actually be counted.

They're about seventy five percent Republican. So we printed them late and mailed them late and passed vote count legislation that cut off ballot counting for anything that wasn't received by the date of the election. Sometimes we stored the mailbags in a warehouse until well after the election."

"Those are great ideas," Biden said. "By the way, Mr. President, Fox News is asking what, exactly, we plan to do about the energy crisis?"

"Oh, come on, Joe," Obama said. "As long as we're in office there is no energy crisis. Energy crises only occur when Republicans are in the White House. You have to tell them that because oil prices are up we're moving as aggressively as possible to green technology. We're developing green companies that are producing green technology and green energy to generate green jobs."

"Well, Mr. President," Biden said, "the guys at Fox are saying that if we don't start doing something now we won't be able to stop inflation from oil prices. They're also saying that you actually want energy price inflation because at today's prices of one hundred dollars a barrel or more oil is still much cheaper than solar energy."

"Geeze, I hate talking to those Fox buttheads," Obama said. "Let me think…Okay, I got it. Tell 'em we're talking to Pickens and Buffet and our other energy team members to come out with a plan."

"Don't we already have a plan?" Biden asked.

"It needs some tweaking."

"Tweaking, sir?"

"Yeah," Obama said. "We have to write it."

Chapter Two

RAHM IT ON IN

"Crime does not pay...as well as politics."

- Alfred E. Newman

"***Rrrrmmmm Drrdddt, Naaaaan Nnnnlllll,***" the intercom crackled.

President Obama looked at Axelrod, Biden, and Daley. Biden and Daley shrugged their shoulders.

Axelrod said, "Sounds like Rahm Emanuel is here, Sir."

"Oh, yeah," Obama said, "he was coming by today." Obama punched the intercom button, "Send in Mr. Emanuel."

"Yyyzzzz, Rrrrssss."

Rahm Emanuel walked into the Oval Office squinting at everybody and reaching out to shake the President's hand. "Mr. President," he said, "how the f*#& are you?"

"Great, Rahm. Good to see you."

"Dave, Bill, Joe...How are you motherf*#&ing criminals doing?"

"Great, Rahm." "Good." "Doing great," they answered simultaneously.

"So what brings you in here from the Windy City, Mayor Emanuel?" Obama asked.

"Well, Barack, I'm here to tell you that I found out that Michelle wants to build a f*#&ing Leadership Academy like Oprah's. Michelle would like for it to be in Chicago, and the boys downtown would like that too."

"A Leadership Academy, huh?" Obama asked. "That's a good idea."

"She wants a lot of f*#&ing money. Chicago could use the project now that we're not getting the f*#&ing Olympics. A lot of the f*#&ing leadership in Chicago was counting on the Olympics."

"The leadership, huh?" Obama asked. "How much are they looking for?"

"Ninety six million was the last f*#&ing number I heard."

"Ninety six million?" Biden asked. "That's all? We ought to be able to do that."

"What can you guys put together for ninety six million?" Obama asked.

"Oh, for ninety six million we can build a hell of an academy. We should be able to put together a f*#&ing top notch ten room academy schoolhouse with a set of restrooms and a basketball court. We could have a great ribbon cutting before the next presidential election. We could get Oprah to come in from L.A. for the event."

"Does Oprah still go to Chicago much?" Obama asked. "I thought she laid off her HARPO studio staff and kind of shut down."

"Well, she tried to," Rahm answered. "But we reminded her that Chicago is a f*#&ing union town. You can't lay off Chicago union people."

"What if there's no work?" Axelrod asked.

"What's that f*#&ing got to do with anything? You can't lay off union workers in Chicago. It's that f*#&ing simple, David."

"Okay, then," Obama said. "Ten rooms, huh?"

"Maybe twelve, but that's pushing things. Good real estate is still expensive in Chicago."

Obama looked at David Axelrod. "How much campaign money do we have right now?"

"About ninety six million," Axelrod said.

Obama pondered this for a few seconds. "Joe, tell the NSA that I want somebody listening in whenever Michelle and Oprah are talking. Tell the Secret Service, too."

"Yes, sir, Mr. President," Biden said.

"Also find out if there's still some unobligated Stimulus Plan money lying around that we can divert to Chicago."

"Yes, sir."

"We'll get word to you about the money, Rahm."

"Wait. Did you say you'll f*#&ing get word to me?!" Emanuel yelled. His eyes bugged out, his face reddened. Emanuel's carotids started bulging and pulsing on both sides of his neck. "If I f*#&ing go back to Chicago with 'they'll get back to me' they'll tear my f*#&ing head off and spit down the goddamned hole. I need a f*#&ing check and I need it f*#&ing now!!! Rezko and Ayers need the money to lay the legal ground work and get permits going."

"Legal groundwork?" Obama asked. "What legal groundwork are you talking about?"

"Rezko and Ayers need to get some indictments spiked and some people f*#&ing taken care of. That'll grease the skids for the project to f*#&ing move forward."

"Okay, okay, Rahm. We'll get the money put together. Give us a couple of days, huh? Isn't Tony in jail, though?" Obama said.

"Yeah, well, that hasn't stopped him from operating. By the way, we have some additional f*#&ing things we need," Rahm said.

"Anything for you Rahm," Obama said. "My heart's always in Chicago."

"Yeah, well, we could use some kind of big f*#&ing Federal project. I'm thinking we could put the Defense Department's new retirement home for Gay and Lesbian Service People there."

"We're building a home for retired gay service members?" Biden asked.

"We f*#&ing should. Those people have gone through f*#&ing hell and deserve some consideration. Besides, Rezko needs some f*#&ing project money. A couple hundred million ought to do it. He can paint out some of his old abandoned housing project buildings. They'll be great homes for retirees for a couple of years. He also might be able to buy some of his sentence off – cut it down to a couple of weeks or so. Hell, Lohan's been able to stay out of jail, why can't he? Jails are overcrowded. He's not a threat to the community. The guy creates jobs, for f*#&'s sake."

"Okay, Rahm," Obama said. "I'll have David and the guys get to work on that."

"One more thing, Barack," Emanuel said, "we have a proposal for a major f*#&ing health care initiative that we'd like to start in Chicago." Emanuel pulled a thick binder out of his briefcase and dropped it on the President's desk.

"So what's this, Rahm?"

"It's a proposal we have to open clinics and put a doctor on every block."

"That's a great idea, Mr. President," Biden said.

"A doctor on every block?" Obama asked. "Isn't that way too expensive?"

"There are some f*#&ing costs involved," Emanuel answered, "but, this way there's access for everybody."

"What if you don't like the doctor on your block?" Biden asked.

"You'd have to move," Emanuel said. "But the doctor-on-every-block idea is a great idea that would f*#&ing pay for itself, Mr. President."

"How's that, Rahm?" Daley asked.

"The doctors would report to us when people died. That way we could stop sending military retirement checks and Social Security checks to f*#&ing dead people."

"How would the doctors know if somebody died?" Obama asked.

"Well, we could pass a law, Mr. President," Biden said. "People would have to go to their neighborhood doctor in order to die. They wouldn't be allowed to die anywhere else. If they do, their families would have to deliver them to the neighborhood clinic…for verification."

"Interesting ideas, Joe. At any rate," Obama said, "it's good to see you, Rahm."

"You guys, too. Remember, Chicago would like to be the pilot site for the f*#&ing doctor-on-every-block idea and the f*#&ing gay military retirement home."

"Good seeing you again, you slimy lizard," Daley said while shaking hands with Emanuel. "Let us know if there's anything else we can do."

"I just did, motherf*#&er. See you round campus."

Chapter Three

WE SHALL GET TO THE BOTTOM, OR ARE WE THERE ALREADY?

"I have come to the conclusion that politics are too serious a matter to be left to the politicians."

-- *Charles De Gaulle*

"Krrrrrk lllldddrrr, Mmmmttttt Zzzzzzdttt," the intercom blasted.

Obama looked at the intercom speaker hopelessly. "Can anyone fix this goddamned thing?"

Axelrod said, "Sounds like Eric Holder is here, Mr. President."

Obama hit the intercom speaker button. "Let him in, please."

13

"*Sssss zzzzrrr,*" the intercom crackled.

Eric Holder walked into the Oval Office. "Mr. President, Bill, David, Mr. Vice President. How are you all?"

"We're great, Eric," Obama said. "To what do we owe the pleasure?"

"Well, sir, there are a couple of pressing issues we need to talk about."

"I'm sure there are," Obama said. "How are the investigations going?"

"Ours or theirs, sir?" Holder asked.

"Theirs? Oh, yes, theirs," Obama said. "Congress. The congressional investigations. Yes, how are those going?"

"Well, sir. The Fast and Furious investigation is not going well."

"Not going well?"

"No, sir. They're beginning to find out what happened," Holder said.

"That sounds good," Obama said sounding hopeful.

"No, sir," Holder said. "I don't think it's good."

"Shouldn't an investigation find out what happened?" Obama asked.

"I don't think we want that in this case," Holder said.

"Why not?"

"Well we don't want them to know things we don't know," Holder said.

"What is it we don't know?"

"Well, Mr. President," Holder said while groping for the right words, "we don't… uh… exactly… uh… know what happened."

"What do we not know about what happened?" Obama asked.

"Well, sir," Holder said while looking around at everybody in the room, "uh…we don't know what happened to the guns. Well, to all the guns."

"What guns?"

"Well, sir, uh...the operation was designed...uh...intended to track guns that went to Mexico."

"That sounds good."

"Well, Mr. President, we lost track of most of them until they turned up later."

"I see. At least they turned up," Obama said.

"Well, sir, that's not necessarily a good thing. They turned up at murder scenes, and gunfights, and in trucks coming back across the border," Holder said.

"How did we lose track of them?"

"Well, sir," Holder stammered, "we... uh... sold them to dealers who sold them to the cartels. We had tracking devices in the guns, but as we tracked them to the border the cartels, who own the Mexican customs people and who know almost all of our federal agents, they managed to detain all of our people at the border while the guns headed on south."

"But, we could still track them, right?"

"Uh, well, sir we tracked them to a river in northern Mexico."

"A river?"

"Yes, sir." Holder said. "The cartels pulled the tracking devices out of all the guns and buried them in a tributary of the Rio Grande. We got the devices back."

"But the guns were gone?" Obama asked.

"Yes, sir."

"So how'd we ultimately get the guns back?"

"Well, sir, the Mexican government found many of the guns after they'd been abandoned at one of the dumps in Tijuana along with the bodies of a number of unfortunate victims."

"So the guns were used to murder people," Obama said.

"Yes, sir. But now we have solid evidence of the

violence that the cartels are responsible for," Holder said.

"Really? We didn't know that before?" Obama asked.

"Well, we certainly had our suspicions," Holder said, "mainly because of the thousands of victims that turn up every year, but now we have real solid evidence."

Obama rubbed his forehead. "So what is Congress' take on this?"

"Well, sir, Representative Issa says that we don't even qualify to be the gang that can't shoot straight if we can't keep track of our own weapons."

"How are we trying to position this story?" Obama asked the group.

Daley answered, "We're telling the public and Congress that this was a complex intelligence gathering operation that yielded a lot of valuable information."

Obama asked, "Is that selling well?"

"Well, sir, the broadcast networks and the Times and Post are okay with it," Daley said. "Fox and Breitbart are skeptical and they're asking a lot of hard questions."

"Have we been trying to answer them?"

"No, sir, our normal media policy is to respond to mainstream media, CNN, and MSNBC only."

"Okay, Eric. What else have you got?"

"Well, sir, we're going to have our hands full with Solyndra and some other solar panel companies going under."

"Some businesses fail. What's the problem?" Obama asked.

"Well, sir, Representative Issa is saying that Solyndra was a naked backroom lobbyist deal that resulted in contributions to the Democratic Party and bills to the taxpayer. He says the White House didn't do its due diligence and, in fact, enabled a transfer of taxpayer dollars to people who immediately benefitted and made political contributions without many steps in between."

"How are we handling this?" Obama asked.

Daley answered, "We're using a number of tactics here, Mr. President. Executive privilege is one because we're conducting our own investigation."

"We are?" Obama asked.

"Not really, Mr. President," Daley said. "We're also pushing out some old dirt we have on Issa, and doing opposition research on other members of the committee."

"Anything else?"

Axelrod said, "We're selling surplus solar panels from the Solyndra bankruptcy liquidation to benefit the Wounded Warriors foundation. We're selling it as a Stimulus Plan effort that, even though the business failed, is benefitting our troops. We're also working on an angle to donate them to schools. Benefitting troops and kids. Can't miss."

"How many solar panels did Solyndra have after the failure?" Obama asked.

"Several million, I think," Axelrod said.

"Several million?! Did they ever sell any?" Obama asked.

"I don't think so, sir. They actually didn't seem to have a sales force when they failed," Axelrod said.

"No sales force?" Obama asked. "How did they plan to sell their solar panels and other products?"

"They had a website, sir," Axelrod said.

Chapter Four

PARDON ME, BILL

"Politics-- n. Strife of interests masquerading as a contest of principles."

-- Ambrose Bierce,
"The Devil's Dictionary"

"*Zzzzz Lllllll Klllllnnnnn Sssssrrrr Pssssdttt,*" the intercom announced.

Obama shrugged his shoulders and looked at his entourage. David Axelrod, who seemed to have an uncanny ability to interpret the intercom static patterns said, "I believe President Bill Clinton is here to see you, sir."

"Oh, yeah. He is on the schedule. Some campaign strategy discussion, I think," Obama said.

18

Obama walked over to the Oval Office door and opened it himself. Bill Clinton was talking to the President's secretary.

"Well, June," Bill Clinton said, "those pearls really set that suit and that blouse up well. You look great. It's good seeing you again."

"Bill, how's it going?" Obama said and extended his hand.

"Great, Barack." Clinton took Obama's hand and pulled him in for a hug which Obama reciprocated awkwardly. "It's good to see you."

"Come on in," Obama said.

Holder, Axelrod, and Daley exchanged pleasantries with President Clinton.

"Bill, to what do we owe the pleasure?" Obama said.

"Well, Barack," Clinton answered, "I have some ideas for your campaign that should help you out of some of the polling problems that you have."

"That would be welcome, Bill. We're all ears."

"This is pretty powerful stuff. I want to make sure that we keep this among ourselves," Clinton said.

Everyone nodded or said "Sure" to Clinton's request.

"Well, what we're talking about here is a revolutionary message delivery approach. It's all about telling specific categories of people the precise messages that they want to hear."

"Who developed this, Bill?" Obama asked.

"Well, Barack, my foundation has a research arm that worked on this. I've got to tell you the test results are outstanding. It's ready to go into broad application."

"Intriguing. Tell us more," Obama said.

"Well," Clinton said. "we call this High Precision Demographic Communications. We identify specific categories among segments of the voting population and, using social media and internet based communications, deliver the right messages to the right people. It's very powerful and very seductive. It works so well it ought to be illegal."

"How'd your group develop the process?" Obama asked.

"We stumbled across a theory that seemed ready for application to a larger effort like a presidential campaign. The theory is a way of identifying specific categories of people that translate to specific message requirements."

"Where'd this come from, Bill?" Obama asked.

"You'll never believe this, but it was a website selling DVDs for techniques to meet and seduce women."

Everyone sat quietly and let this one sink in a bit.

"The theory is the thing, though. We won't be seducing women, but we will be seducing voters. We'll use some of the same techniques. The first thing you do is ask people three simple questions and by the time they finish answering you'll have the message track you need."

"How did you and your folks test this, Mr. President?" Axelrod asked.

"Oh, David, that's interesting," Clinton said. "I tested it myself. I had the Secret Service bring women over to me and I tested them. It worked. It worked every time. It worked so well I almost got bored with it. Hundreds of them. It's really powerful."

Holder, Axelrod, Daley, and Obama sat with stunned looks on their faces.

"I can apply this to your advantage. You'll get wonderful poll results," Clinton said.

"Well, Bill, how can we make this work? How many categories can there be?" Obama asked.

"Well, theoretically there can be a couple of hundred. Affluent women alone can be put into about seven or eight categories."

"That's a lot. So we have to tailor our messages to appeal to a couple of hundred categories of people? Sounds complicated," Obama said.

"That's the theory, but we don't need to go that far. Think of it this way. You've pretty much got the Blacks and Latinos and Muslim men locked up. The Jews will vote Democratic even if they have to hold their noses. What we've got to do is keep the women in your camp and even increase their numbers. From the numbers I've seen you've lost a lot of independent women if the election were held today."

"That seems to be true today," Obama admitted. "We have a program to work on that."

"Well let me do that for you. I can do that. I need about twelve million," Clinton said.

"Twelve million? Dollars? What are you proposing exactly?" Obama asked.

"We'll send advanced teams into the key swing states and get the women back on your side. My guys go in and establish the categories and I work with the key female leaders in each group to start the turning process."

"When do you need the twelve million?" Obama asked.

"Well, Barack, we need to jump on this right away. This will take time. There are a lot of influential women out there," Clinton said.

"That's true," Obama said.

"If we do this right, you'll have blacks, Latinos, Asians, Muslims, and women in your pocket. You won't need a single white male vote to get re-elected."

Axelrod and Daley raised their eyebrows.

"This is great, Barack," Biden said.

"True, this is a fascinating idea, Bill. I tell you what. David and I will work on lining up the financing. I appreciate you dropping by. We'll get funding to you right away."

"I think you'll be pleased. This will put the election in the bag."

Everybody stood up, shook hands, and said their goodbyes. Clinton walked out the door and immediately started another conversation with June and Aileen, the outer office secretaries.

"Cut a check for three hundred thousand for this, David."

"Yes, sir, but he asked for twelve million," Axelrod said.

"True," Obama said. "He can help us get the rest of it from some of those influential women he's going to…uh…spend time with."

Chapter Five

LOGIC NOTWITHSTANDING

"The problem with political jokes is they get elected."

-- Henry Cate VII

Obama looked around the Oval Office. "Hey guys," Obama asked, "does anybody have any idea what Hillary's up to these days?"

Eric Holder said, "Right after she fell down the Capital steps and broke her tooth, she went on a D.C. Listening Tour. She said she wanted to listen to everybody who works for the Federal Government right here in D.C."

"What?" Obama asked. "She's Secretary of State. She should be overseas."

"She doesn't want to go overseas until she gets her tooth fixed. That's why she's listening instead of talking," Axelrod said.

"Do we know what people are telling her?" Obama asked.

Axelrod said, "One of the things they're telling her, sir, is that if the New York Times and ABC, NBC, and CBS had done their jobs on Edwards she'd be president."

Biden added, "Did we really have to invite Hillary to join the cabinet?"

"Joe, the Democratic Party is a big tent. Room for everyone," Obama said with a fairly insincere smile.

Biden answered, "I'm not sure it's that big. A friend of mine over at Defense called to say she paid a visit to let them know they work for her."

"Really?" Daley said. "Next thing you know she'll claim Health and Human Services is part of the State Department."

"Sebelius said that she's already been over there," Biden said.

"David, could you get one of our people to tag along with her?" Obama asked "Does anybody know where she's going today?"

Axelrod said, "She's over at Homeland Security this morning and visiting the Fed this afternoon."

"Eric, get somebody going on this from a legal perspective. Maybe you should look into it yourself," Obama said.

"Yes, sir, Mr. President," Holder responded.

"I'm thinking that some of our problems with Hillary have to do with message discipline. Joe, you and I need to get straight on some our messages. When you and I are out talking we need to be saying the same things."

"Good idea, Mr. President. I know where we could

start," Biden said. "I've got to tell you I'm not sure I understand the financial bailout plan."

"I know, Joe. It took me a while to figure it out, but it's pretty simple really. We give money to banks to lend to people."

"That part I got," Biden said, "but what about the automobile industry?"

"We gave them money to keep operations going and keep union members employed."

"That's what confuses me," Biden said. "I've been asked by the media a number of times about who gives us money."

"The taxpayers give us the money, Joe…Republicans, mainly."

"Wow, I like that idea," Biden said.

"I do too, Joe," Obama said. "But, I've been thinking that we're still not getting our message out there. We need to go on a kind of Listening Tour of our own."

"That's a great idea," Biden said. "I love to listen when I'm not talking."

"But, we need to call it something else," Obama said. "Hillary already used 'listening tour' when she ran for Senator. We don't want to be accused of just copying Hillary."

"How about a 'thinking tour'?" Biden asked.

"Hmmm. Sounds pretty quiet," Obama said.

"What about a 'think and talk' tour or a 'talk and think' tour?" Biden asked.

"When do we think and when do we talk?" Obama asked.

"We'll talk most of the time and we'll think while the other guy is talking," Biden said.

"Hmmm, let me think about that. We probably need to call it something else," Obama said.

"Do we need to take Pelosi along this time?" Biden

asked. "Her approvals are in the basement and sometimes the things she says don't seem...I don't know...very smart."

"We've been talking about that, Joe. David and I agree that we need to distance ourselves from her," Obama said.

"Maybe that's the best reason for going on the tour... to get away from her."

"Sssssttttt Dddddnnnnnt," the intercom blared, *"tttttttttttt mmmmnnnnn sssseeeee pllllllllllllssssss."*

Obama glanced at Axelrod. "Uh, Mr. President, Congresswoman Pelosi is on the phone, I think," Axelrod said.

"Wow. We must be psychic. Okay, I'll take it."

Pelosi's voice came through the speaker phone. "Mr. President, how are you?"

"Couldn't be better, Madam Speaker. What can I do for you?"

"I need some help with the C.I.A. Before we get there, though, could I ask you please not to call me 'Madam' anymore? Since Barbara Boxer unloaded on that general we women all have to line up and be consistent. 'Madam' sounds old or sounds like some kind of owner of a brothel. Besides, I'm not the Speaker of the House now."

"I'll try to remember that, Congresswoman Pelosi. Now, what's up with the C.I.A.?"

"Well, Petraeus over there is just not playing along" Pelosi said. "We're trying to ram a poker up the Bush administration's ass with the water torture thing and he's saying I knew all about it."

"As I recall, and I'm just trying to remember the details Congresswoman Pelosi, but you were briefed on the water boarding technique and its planned application. By the way, with the Democratic Party not being in the majority anymore in the House I can't help but wonder about what you can do at this time about this torture issue."

"Well, Mr. President," Pelosi said, "first of all, my staff members were briefed and my chief of staff briefed me. And secondly we want to open an Attorney General's investigation into the torture allegations. He still works for us doesn't he?"

"He does work for us. But let's get back to the briefing issue. You were briefed were you not?"

"Mr. President, I was not briefed by the C.I.A. I was briefed by my staff."

"Honestly, I don't understand," Obama said. "But, you knew about the water boarding, didn't you?"

"Mr. President, it's like anything else with the Bush administration. They briefed you on stuff, and then they actually went and did what they said they were going to do. Nobody believed they'd actually do what they said they were going to do. Besides, I was going in for an adjustment that day and was distracted."

"An adjustment?"

"Yes, Mr. President, my surgeon was tightening up my jaw line in the afternoon. It was beginning to show some sagging in profile shots."

"I hadn't noticed that, Congresswoman."

"Well, thank you. He does good work. He's in Beverly Hills. He does Joan Rivers from time to time. A couple of times a year, I think."

"I see," Obama said. "So let me make sure I understand this. You were in California and were debriefed by your staff. Is that right?"

"Yes. So you see, Mr. President, I couldn't possibly remember that the C.I.A. actually briefed the water boarding thing with any real idea that they would actually use it."

"Well, Congresswoman Pelosi, I'll call David and see what's going on, but you may have to issue a statement about your own scheduling problems that day."

"Thank you, Mr. President. Could I trouble you with one other thing?" Pelosi asked.

"Sure."

"We're thinking of starting up a campaign against having too many children. We want to release some ads."

"Too many children?" Obama asked. "What will your ads say?"

"Our test ads let people know how much an average child costs," Pelosi said.

"How much they cost? You're telling people how much it costs to have children?"

"Yes, Mr. President. Children cost money and that cuts down on our tax revenue," Pelosi continued. "You know – the number of exemptions and all that."

"Well, I don't do my own taxes," Obama said. "So I'm not sure what exactly you're planning on telling people."

"We're telling them that children represent costs and we need to cut down on costs. You know what's going on with the budget. I think the Budget Super Committee looked at the idea of cutting down on the number of children in the country."

"Really?" Obama asked. "I didn't hear that they had looked at that idea. Anyway, if people stop having children where will we get voters and people to serve in the military?"

"Oh, Mr. President, we get enough voters and enough soldiers from immigration."

"Are you saying that we're winning wars and winning elections because illegal immigrants are voting for us?

"Mr. President, there are no illegal immigrants. At least, that's what our next bill will say."

"What bill is that?"

Pelosi said, "We're calling it the 'Two Weeks Feet Dry' bill. If you get to the United States, and you get a receipt from a MacDonald's or something to prove you got here, and you manage to evade the INS for over two weeks you are home free. We're asking you to please sign the bill next week when it hits your desk."

"We'll have a look at it, Congresswoman Pelosi. Thank you."

"We've got one other bill we would like you to consider signing, Mr. President," Pelosi said.

"Okay, what is this one?" Obama asked.

"It's the Buffet Subsidy Bill."

"A buffet subsidy bill?" Obama asked.

"Yes, Mr. President," Pelosi answered. "Everybody knows that people who eat at buffets consume a lot more calories and don't live as long. We think this should be part of our plan to cut down on Social Security and Medicare benefits. By subsidizing buffets, people will die sooner. Less benefit money is paid out."

"But won't this idea disable more people?" Obama asked. "We'll have to pay for their hospitalization."

"We'll subsidize buffets in hospitals and rest homes and encourage the people there to eat a lot. That way their lives will be cut short. We'll save on costs and while they're killing themselves with food they'll eat like kings and queens. Farmers and food producers will sell more food. It's a win-win situation."

"Well, okay Congresswoman Pelosi, we'll look at that bill too."

"Thank you, and good bye, Mr. President. Say 'hello' to Michelle for me."

President Obama disconnects the call.

"That woman's going to cause us problems," Biden said.

Chapter Six

DEEP COVER UNDERCOVER

"When the political columnists say 'Every thinking man' they mean themselves, and when candidates appeal to 'Every intelligent voter' they mean everybody who is going to vote for them."

- *Franklin P. Adams*

    David Axelrod cleared his throat and said, "Mr. President, I have an issue we need to talk about."
    "What's that, David," Obama asked.
    "I have to tell you, sir, that the Republicans are showing a few signs of life."
    "What do you mean, David? I thought we had them in a box," Biden said.
    "We do, Mr. Vice President, sort of," Axelrod said,

"but they have some ideas."

"Ideas?" Obama asked. "What kind of ideas?"

"Well, we've been told that they're starting up an ad campaign."

"An ad campaign?" Obama asked. "It's kind of early to be spending a lot of media money. What kind of ad campaign are they running?"

"Well, Mr. President," Axelrod said, "we're not sure exactly. Some of our spies said they couldn't get themselves invited into the super secret meetings."

"Super secret meetings?!" Biden asked.

"Yes, Mr. Vice President. Unlike our party, the Republicans occasionally figure out how to keep a secret."

"Well, how pray tell do they do that?" Biden asked.

"They just…uh…they don't tell anybody anything …outside their group, that is."

Biden talked with a measure of urgency in his voice, "What? They don't tell anybody? How can you have an idea and not tell anybody? I tell everybody all of my ideas."

"Yes, Mr. Vice President," Axelrod said, "I understand. But, the Republicans don't always do that."

"Well, then," Biden asked, "just how are they going to get anywhere with an idea if they don't tell anybody?"

"Well," Axelrod continued, "they'll tell everybody soon, but they'll pick the time and place to get the word out. They'll tell Fox News first."

"Fox News?" Obama asked. "Just what do you think they'll tell Fox News?"

"We don't know exactly, Mr. President, but we have an idea," Axelrod said.

"Care to share it?" Obama asked.

"Yes, sir," Axelrod said, "but just so you know the source may not be reliable."

"Who's the source?"

"Mr. President, I don't know his name. My source tells me that his source has a source he calls Deep Tongue."

"Deep Tongue?" Obama asked. "You're kidding."

"No, sir."

"I've heard of Deep Tongue too, sir," Biden said.

"Well, what is Deep Tongue allegedly saying?" Obama asked.

"He, or she, is basically saying that the Republican campaign will acknowledge that you're a great guy and you're family is lovely. But, the ad will claim that you're surrounded by activists, left-leaning enablers, and idiots who never passed basic math."

"What??" Obama asked.

"Your advisors and Congress...they've got to go. They don't know how to stop spending money they don't have."

"All of them have to go??"

"Sir," Axelrod said, "I'm not saying they've all got to go. The Republican ads will say that."

"Is this true?"

"What's that, sir?" Axelrod said.

"That I'm surrounded by those kinds of people?" Obama asked.

"Let's give 'em all a math test, Mr. President," Biden said, "and publish the results."

"David, seriously," Obama asked, "do you think all the people around me are idiots?"

"No, sir, Mr. President. Not all of them." Axelrod paused for a second to reflect on how he phrased his last response. "On a related note I think we need a new poll, sir."

"Won't a new poll just show us the same results?"

"Not necessarily, sir," Axelrod answered. "We can push an external poll out pretty quickly."

"Push an external poll out?" Obama asked. "What does that mean?"

"Mr. President, we have an internal polling group that can put out an instant poll using their continuous polling and extrapolation techniques."

"How do they do that?"

"Well, sir," Axelrod said, "they use polling data that they collect every day and then they apply derivative processing to extend the results using projection algorithms and data mining techniques. They apply historic data and then they filter the anomalies."

"Do the news outlets use what we give them from this kind of polling?" Obama asked.

"The broadcast networks and the L.A. and New York Times are good with it. So are CNN and MSNBC. Fox and Breitbart ask a lot of questions though."

"Fascinating," Obama said. "Tell me more about this filtering thing they do. How do they filter out the 'anomalies' that you mentioned?"

"Well, sir, they eliminate any responses from fringe group members like the Republican Party or people who claim to be Tea Party members."

"I see. I suppose that makes sense to cut down on bias," Obama said.

"True, sir. And as a result of their exclusive and highly sophisticated technology their processing can predict what a larger sample would be," Axelrod said.

"Isn't it true that pollsters generally don't use large samples? What's the difference between what our group does and what other polling groups do now?"

"Well, sir," Axelrod said, "nothing really, except with our techniques the sample size can be extremely small."

"How small is an extremely small sample, David?" Obama asked.

"About ten people, sir," Axelrod said. "They often just use the people in their own office."

Chapter Seven

**BRIDGES AND ROADS,
ROADS AND BRIDGES**

"The word 'politics' is derived from the word 'poly', meaning 'many', and the word 'ticks', meaning 'blood sucking parasites'."

- *Larry Hardiman*

"Sssssnnn Rrrrrddddd," the intercom crackled, *"Nnnnnrrrr pppppppdddddd nnndd ssssss rrrrrgggggnn."*

Obama looked at Axelrod who seemed to be struggling with this one.

"Senator Reid is on the phone, Mr. President," Axelrod said. "At least I think that's what she said."

"I'll take it," Obama said into the intercom. "Harry,

how are you today?"

"Okay, so far, Mr. President, but we've got to talk about health care," Reid said.

"Let's do that, Harry. I just want you to know you're on a speaker phone with Bill Daley, David Axelrod, Vice President Biden, and Attorney General Eric Holder."

"Hi, guys. It's good having you all listen. Let me give you the short version so that when we meet we'll all be prepared to talk more productively."

"Great, Harry. Let us hear what you've got."

"Here's the basic idea, Mr. President," Reid said. "As you know coal makes us sick. Oil makes us sick. All fossil fuels make us sick. We're getting sicker and sicker."

"Got it. Go on," Obama said.

"Well, Las Vegas is powered by hydroelectric power from Hoover Dam. People don't get sick there. Is everyone with me so far?"

"I think so, Harry."

"So our proposal is that we move D. C. to Las Vegas and put in high speed rail transit from Vegas to L.A., New York, and Chicago."

"We move D. C. to Las Vegas?" Obama asked.

"Yes sir, Mr. President. We've got clean power. The weather's better. You'll demonstrate your commitment to a clean environment. Heck, maybe we can actually double or triple our federal revenue by betting the budget money in the casinos."

"Wow, Senator Reid," Obama said, "that's a pretty interesting set of ideas. Can you help me out a bit and relate that back to health care again?"

"Well, Mr. President, moving D.C. to Vegas would mean fewer people in the Potomac area. Fewer colds. Fewer people getting sick because of coal and oil. Burning less fossil fuels, you know. It'll just be healthier."

"Okay, Harry, I think I get it now. Well, thank you for sharing your ideas. I look forward to talking to you about this."

"Thank you, Mr. President. Have a nice day."

Obama disconnected the call. "Well, David, where were we? Does this Deep Tongue have anything else?"

"Just that it's the first phase of a three part campaign."

"What are the other two phases?" Obama asked.

"We don't know that yet, Mr. President," Axelrod said. "There is another issue that we should talk about, however."

"What's that?"

"Sir, we need to talk about Dorothy, the beauty shop owner from Springfield."

"Who's that?" Obama asked.

"She's been on Fox News, Breitbart's website, and Drudge Report claiming the Stimulus Bill has failed to help small business."

"What does she mean it's failed?" Obama asked. "How could it have failed? What's she saying?"

Axelrod said, "Well, sir, She claims Vice President Biden's office could not tell her one thing that the Stimulus Bill is doing that helps small business. She's adamant and fairly convincing."

"Joe, do you know anything about this?" Obama asked.

"Mr. President," Biden said, "I don't know how she figures it. The Stimulus Plan has to be helping her. We're fixing roads and bridges. She needs those things for people to get to her business. Bridges. Roads. Bridges. She needs 'em, right? Roads?"

"Well…uh…Mr. Vice President," Axelrod said, "she says the roads and bridges she has near her business are fine. They don't need fixing and they don't need new ones. On Fox News she said, 'If that's the best you've got I'm going

Republican'."

Obama hit his intercom button and said, "Could you ask Mr. Carney to come to my office, please?"

"*Yyxxxx sssss,*" the intercom hissed.

Obama released the intercom button and said, "What do we do about this?"

"We should audit her, Mr. President," Axelrod said. "There isn't a small business on the planet that hasn't cheated or made a mistake on their taxes. Let's do a Joe the Plumber on her."

"*Sssssrrrt Pppnnnnnt,*" the intercom hissed, "*Nnnrrr Gggggssss izzzzz heeeee.*"

Obama looked at Axelrod. "I think I've got this one. Carney is here, right?"

"Yes, sir," Axelrod replied.

Obama hit the intercom button, "Send him in."

"*Zzzzzzz Rrrrrrrr,*" the intercom popped.

Jay Carney walked into the room "Thank you for calling me down here, Mr. President. The press corps was hounding me about Iran and Fast and Furious again."

"Jay, how are you doing?" Obama asked. "We'll send you back to the press corps soon, but right now we need to know something. Just what do you know about Dorothy, the beauty shop owner from Springfield?"

"Well, Mr. President," Carney said, "She's popping off to right wing media about the Stimulus Bill not doing anything for small business."

"Do you have any ideas on mitigating this?"

Carney thought for a second and said, "We could take her on. Frankly, I think this is small enough that we should sympathize and tell her we will see what we can do."

"I tend to agree. Let's not run the audit yet, David. Joe, is there any way we can reach out to her? Maybe we can turn this into a photo op."

"We'll try, Mr. President," Biden said.

"What are we going to tell her?" Axelrod asked looking directly at Biden.

"Well, David," Biden said, "I'd just remind her that even though she doesn't think much of what we're doing to bridges and roads, she needs those things to run her business. We should tell her about the great websites we have for the Stimulus package with all the pictures of bridges and roads, and recommend that she check out the website for the Small Business Administration. And in order to really help her, I'm sure we can help her union employees with some bailout money."

"Mr. Vice President, she's got two employees. They're not unionized."

"Well heck, David, we can help with that, too. We'll ask the AFL-CIO or the ACORN folks to head on over there and organize her people. She's in Illinois, right?"

"No, sir," Axelrod said. "Springfield, Texas."

The words 'dumb struck' hardly seemed adequate. Finally, Obama recovered long enough to ask, "How in the hell is any major media event like this coming out of Texas? They don't have any media down there, do they? Who listens to people from Texas? Surely there's some story we can push up to our friends at the Times and at CNN to drown this thing out."

"I'm not so sure, sir," Axelrod said. "It seems as though a large number of reporters that had been pulled out of Iran and Afghanistan were laid off, for the most part, due to budget cutting at mainstream news outlets. A lot of them decided they didn't really want to live in Washington, New York, Chicago, or California. Many of them moved to Texas to become independent journalists…bloggers so to speak."

"Bloggers," Biden said. "I hate bloggers."

"These bloggers seem to have gotten organized,"

Axelrod said. "They write pretty good pieces, and they've begun to give more visibility to stories out of Texas. They're getting a lot of play, and other news organizations are picking up their stories."

"So these are the people who are reporting on this Dorothy woman?" Obama asked.

"Initially," Axelrod said. "Fox picked the story up and so did Breitbart and Drudge. Eventually all the outlets carried something on it."

"Drudge," Biden said and started laughing. "Sounds like 'sludge' doesn't it?" Biden kept laughing while everybody else stayed quiet. Biden eventually settled down.

"Okay, here's what we're going to do," Obama said. "Bill, call Panetta and see if there are any other high profile terrorists we can knock off easily. Maybe we can release one from Guantanamo, track him as he leaves, and hit him right after he gets back to Pakistan. David, let's act like we're on the side of small business. Call this woman and ask her if she'd like to come to the White House and have a beer with me in the Rose Garden."

"She doesn't drink beer, Mr. President," Axelrod said. "She's made a big point of that in all of her interviews. Texas Bible thumper. I recommend tea, sir."

"Can we make it coffee?"

"She doesn't drink coffee either. Health kick. Green tea, sir. Green tea."

"Blecchh. Okay, see if she'll bite on that. Bill, see if you can find some leftover Stimulus money to help her to expand her business. David, let's get some kind of story to crowd this out of the news. Whatever you've got. An oil spill, or a hurricane, or an earthquake, or something."

Obama looks around the room at the group. "Everyone got it?"

"What do you want me to do?" Biden asked.

"You're the Vice President, Joe. You need to stay above this," Obama said.

"Right," Biden said as if he actually understood.

Chapter Eight

THREAT MATRIX

"Politics is not a bad profession. If you succeed there are many rewards. If you disgrace yourself you can always write a book."

- Ronald Reagan

"Sssssnnn Rrrrrddddd," the intercom crackled, **"Nnnnnrrrr ppppppdddddd nnndd sssss rrrrrggggnn."**

"Mr. President," Axelrod said, "it sounds like Secretary Napolitano is on the phone. I believe she said it was urgent."

"Okay, put her through," Obama said.

Janet Napolitano's voice came over the speaker phone, "Mr. President, I'm sorry to interrupt, but my people have called an urgent matter to my attention."

"What's that, Madam...uh... Secretary Napolitano?" Obama asked.

"Am I on speaker phone, sir?"

"Oh, yes you are. Bill Daley, Joe Biden, David Axelrod, and Eric Holder are here."

"I see," Napolitano said. "Well, gentlemen, as some of you know we've engaged with the University of Illinois Center for Terrorism Studies to evaluate the threat profile of every possible group or major public figure or leader in the world. They've compiled the largest database of this information anywhere and have conducted extensive modeling and analysis."

"And what they turned up?" Obama asked.

"Well, as you know, Mr. President, there are a number of significant threats external to the United States that are well known – terrorist networks, rogue regimes, narco-terrorist cartels, organized international crime. However, the biggest threat to the stability of our country and our government is within. It is among our very own domestic dissident elements. The biggest threats, according to the Center's analysis, are talk radio and Fox News."

"Wait, wait," Obama said. "What about the Iranians with nukes, Secretary Napolitano? What about North Korea, the Russians, radical Muslims, the Cubans, South America, Somalia? What are they really saying?"

"What they're saying, Mr. President, is that Hugh Hewitt, Michael Medved, Roger Hedgecock, Dennis Prager, Rush Limbaugh, Glenn Beck, Ann Coulter, Sean Hannity, and Bill O'Reilly are bigger, more potent threats. They have the power to incite significant domestic resistance."

"Resistance?" Obama asked. "Resistance to what?"

"Resistance, Mr. President," Napolitano said. "Resistance to everything that needs to be done. Resistance to abortion rights, the NGLTB agenda, gays in the military, reparations, nationalized health care, public transportation initiatives like high-speed rail, reduced executive compensation, unionization, Cap and Trade taxation...you name it."

"Secretary Napolitano, is the Center recommending that we go to war with these people?" Obama asked.

"Oh, no sir, Mr. President. But, my advisors say they should be under 24/7 surveillance."

"Based on what?"

"Well, sir," Napolitano said, "based on the results of our analysis. It amounts to a threat assessment. They represent a clear and present danger."

"Where did this come from, Secretary Napolitano?"

"Well, we had some consultants affiliated with Harvard and MIT work with the University of Illinois to develop a massive database analysis program with a scanning and search capability. This system is tightly coupled with pattern recognition software, large scale historical databases, and advanced threat processing algorithms."

"Have I heard of this program? What is it called?"

"Mr. President, the developers call their program the Continuous Realtime Algorithmic Processor for Linear Orthogonal Analysis of Data."

"Wow, that's a mouthful. Does the program have a short name?"

"Uh, yes sir. The acronym for the program which is...uh... derived from the first letter of each word in the title..."

"Secretary Napolitano, I know what an acronym is."

"Uh, yes sir. Well the acronym for this program is... uh, it's CRAPLOAD, sir."

"CRAPLOAD?"

"Yes, sir. CRAPLOAD."

"You guys couldn't come up with anything better than CRAPLOAD?"

"Sir, we didn't name it. The academics at Harvard and MIT came up with the name."

"Secretary Napolitano," Obama said. "I'll get back to you on this. Is there anything else?"

"Yes, sir. One other thing. I took care of that tax problem," Napolitano said.

"What tax problem? You had an income tax issue at one time as I recall."

"No sir, not income tax. A reporter found out that I bought Nutrisystem on the Internet and I hadn't paid a state sales tax on it. I sent the check in right away."

"Does Fox News know about this?" Obama asked.

"I don't think so, Mr. President. This was uncovered by some blogger kind of reporter. She says she hates Fox News."

"Good."

"Yes, sir," Napolitano said. "She also says she hates the Tea Party, the Democratic Party, ABC, CBS, NBC, MSNBC, CNN, the Republican Party, vegetarians, meat eaters, global warming, global cooling, climate change, climates that don't change, the New York Times, the Washington Post, and Arianna Huffington. Strangely, she does like Rush Limbaugh, though."

"I see. Interesting mix," Obama said. "Let me know if anything changes on this."

"Yes sir, Mr. President. Thank you."

Chapter Nine

SEEKING TRUTH

"In politics you must always keep running with the pack. The moment that you falter and they sense that you are injured, the rest will turn on you like wolves."
- R. A. Butler

Obama looked around at the group. "We've got to get out of here." Obama punched up his intercom. "Alert the Secret Service that we're going out in 30 minutes. Have them get cars ready."

"Xxxxxxx Rsssssss," the speaker blared.

"David. Joe. We're going on a Fact Finding Trip," Obama announced.

"Fact finding?" Biden asked.

"Yep, Joe. We're going in search of the Stimulus funding. We're going to find out who got it and what's happening with it. So, can you get me a list of local organizations who received money from the Stimulus plan?"

"Yes, sir," Biden said.

After about forty five minutes Obama is sitting in the back seat of a black government Suburban SUV. Biden and Axelrod are in the back seat riding with him as he reads a list.

Biden said, "I'd feel better out here if I had a weapon of some kind."

"Relax, Joe," Obama said. "We have the Secret Service here. I trust them."

"That's right, Mr. President," Biden said "'When seconds count, they're only minutes away'. I heard that on a Fox News gun rights special."

"Joe, the Secret Service is here. They're right here with us. Kick back a little bit."

"I'm sorry, Mr. President. I'm a little jumpy. I guess I was embarrassed that the list was so small."

"Yeah, I wonder about this. Something's wrong with this database, I think," Obama said. "It looks like the only places getting Stimulus money in D. C. are Americorps, a bagel shop, and some community organizing group called 'MAGA'. Does anybody know what MAGA is?"

"Well, sir," Axelrod said, "MAGA is a great group. MAGA stands for Making ACORN Grab America. They help poor people get loans."

"That's good. How do they help the poor people pay the loans back?" Obama asked.

"They don't have to," Biden said, "the loans are government guaranteed."

Obama thought about that for a second.

"I know there are more places in the Washington area getting Stimulus funding, Mr. President," Biden said. "Heck, most of the money was supposed to be spent in Washington. It just takes a while for my guys to get the data over to my web site number."

Obama thought about this for a second. "It's okay for now, Joe. We'll make this work. I like Americorps. Clinton invented that. Let's go to their office."

"Yeah," Biden said, "Americorps is a good organization. We've been able to get them to register a lot of Democrats and campaign for a lot of candidates."

"Whoa, Joe. Hang on," Obama said. "David, I don't understand. Does Americorps do this using federal funds?"

"Oh, no, Mr. President," Axelrod said. "Americorps firewalls the federal funds from any use in campaign activities. The young people support the campaigning effort because they're motivated to make a difference."

"Of course they are," Obama said. "Americorps is full of energetic young people who really work hard. I am a little concerned, however. Just how did they set up this accounting firewall you described, David?"

"Well, sir," David said, "they hired over forty attorneys and accountants to set up an audit proof set of books and databases that cannot possibly be deciphered to infer any use of federal funds in campaign activity."

"I see," Obama said. "And just what is their funding source for paying young people to participate in the democratic process?"

"Well, sir, George Soros lends money to Americorps, so they will have the funds to pay people who work on campaign support activities."

"He lends money?"

"Yes, sir. Millions."

"And does he expect to be paid back?"

"Why yes, sir. It's a loan."

"What kind of interest rate do we pay him?"

"I think it's on the order of twelve percent, sir."

The President's car was hit suddenly in the rear quarter panel by another black Chevy Suburban SUV. Two caravans of black Chevy Suburban SUV's had collided in a massive six SUV pileup. The collisions were relatively minor and there were no serious injuries.

Heavily armed Secret Service personnel emerged from the presidential caravan SUVs and pointed guns in the general direction of the other group of SUVs. Heavily armed body guards in hooded sweatshirts with lots of bling, flat billed baseball caps, and chrome plated semiautomatic hand guns poured out of the other SUVs and pointed their guns in the general direction of the Secret Service Agents.

"Hands up! Lay down your weapons!" the agents repeated.

"Drop 'em or me and my homies'll cap you!!"

"Hands up!"

"Lay 'em down, cracker!"

"Hands up and lay down your arms!!" the agents repeated.

"We'll put your sorry white butts in the ground!"

"One last warning!!! Hands up!!! Lay your weapons down."

"JayLo ain't gonna let us drop our guns! D.C.'s too dangerous!!"

Obama rolled down his window and stuck his head out. "Did you say 'JayLo'? Jennifer Lopez?"

One of the bodyguards recognized the President. "Mr. President??"

"Yes, it's me."

"Well, Mr. Prez, JayLo was coming to see you."

"She was?"

"Yes, sir."

"Okay," Obama said. "Before anybody does anything

stupid, can we all lower the weapons?"

Hesitantly, JayLo's bodyguards slowly lower their weapons as does the Secret Service.

"You said that Jennifer Lopez was coming to see me?"

"Yes, sir."

Obama looks back in the car at Daley. "Was she on the schedule?"

"No, sir" Daley said. "Not my copy anyway."

Obama looks back out the window. "I tell you what. Miss Lopez can meet me now while we sort out this collision and determine which vehicles are still in working order."

Lopez's bodyguard said, "Uh, okay, President Obama. I'll tell her." He walked back to one of the Lopez SUVs and opened the door to talk to the occupants. Finally, Jennifer Lopez came out of the car escorted by Ryan Reynolds.

She was talking on her cell phone as she walked up to President Obama's car. "I don't care, Tony, you schmuck. You agreed that you would take the kids this weekend. I'll see you Friday afternoon at 3 pm. That's it! Do it!"

Jennifer Lopez looked into the presidential SUV and said, "Mr. President, it is indeed an honor. I'm Jennifer Lopez and this is Ryan Reynolds." They were both dressed in jeans, sandals, and sweatshirts.

Obama said, "I know who you are, Miss Lopez. Please come in and have a seat. Ryan, you too."

"Thank you, sir." Lopez and Reynolds climbed into the back seat of the SUV.

Obama introduced everyone to each other and then said, "It's a pleasure to meet the two of you. Ryan, I liked that *Green Hornet* picture you were in this year."

"Uh, that was, uh, *Green Lantern*, sir, Mr. President," Ryan mumbled.

"Ah, that's right, Mr. Reynolds. Getting my 'greens' mixed up. Sorry. And Ms. Lopez, I understand you were on your way to see me. What can I do for you?"

"Well, Mr. President," Lopez began, "there's a crisis in my business. Show business and media, I mean. There's a problem that needs to be solved and I would like to talk to you about some laws to help us out."

"A crisis in show business? I hadn't heard. What kind of crisis?"

"Well, sir" Lopez said, "it takes some explaining but basically the nation is being victimized by untalented people."

"Untalented people?" Obama asked.

"Yes sir. It started with *Survivor*, the first really huge reality show. Then came a stream of things like *Real World* on *MTV*, *Jersey Shore*, and *The Bachelor*."

"Well, Miss Lopez," Obama said, "I'm aware of these shows, but I wasn't aware of a crisis."

"Oh, but Mr. President," Lopez pleaded, "it's very serious. People with no talent are getting all the air time, the magazine covers, and the entertainment news exposure. People who can't sing, dance, or act are all over the place. They're sucking all the oxygen out of the business. Our nation's entertainment industry is threatened. Some of these reality people like that Snooki chick have higher name recognition than I do."

"I see," Obama said. "I suppose there is a problem of some kind there."

"Mr. President," Lopez said, "it's worse than you think. Where young people used to want to grow up and sing, dance, or act, now they just want to get a reality show. They don't want to practice their songs or rehearse lines or learn their moves. They just want to make it up while some video camera rolls on."

"Hmmm," Obama said.

"Sir, it's all come to a head with that Kardashian chick and her family. She was on every cover and every news program sucking up all the publicity machinery and nobody else could get a word in edgewise. She gets publicity for her family's little arguments, for her wedding, for her divorce, and for her next boyfriend. She gets publicity when she farts, for God's sake! She does absolutely nothing! Nothing! She was on *Dancing With the Stars* for five weeks before people finally voted her off for not moving her feet, her butt, or her face. And now her mom just runs around and gets on every talk show on the planet to talk about how sincere she was about being married and how she wants to have a baby. Having a baby doesn't require any talent! Give me a break!"

"It does sound like there's a problem there," Obama said. "But, I don't know how I can help."

"President Obama, we need legislation," Lopez said forcefully.

"We do?"

"Yes, sir, we do," Lopez said.

"What kind of legislation?" Obama asked.

"Well, sir, we need to separate entertainment from reality. We need legislation to separate the media that covers reality programming and reporting from legitimate entertainment media like *Entertainment Weekly* and *Entertainment Tonight*. You know – the television show. We need laws to prevent entertainment media from reporting on reality shows and reality show people. They should have their own media. They can't steal ours."

"Hmmm. Well, I have a question, Miss Lopez," Obama said. "You are a judge on what some people would call a reality program – *American Idol*. With this kind of law the entertainment media couldn't report on your involvement in that program because it's a reality program, right?"

"Mr. President," Lopez said, "*American Idol* is not a reality program. It's an entertainment program with music and singing."

"Yes, but the Emmy awards categorize it as a reality show, don't they?" Obama asked.

"Well, sir, we can get that changed."

"I see," Obama said. "Well, Miss Lopez, have someone write up a legislative proposal and send it to Representative Boehner, the Speaker of the House, and we'll see if we can schedule it for a debate."

"Write it up? This is a crisis, Mr. President. Can't we get an executive order or something?" Lopez asked.

"I'm not sure, Miss Lopez, that I can work it that way," Obama said. "Executive orders are for governmental functions that are specifically enumerated in the Constitution. I'm not sure that oversight over the entertainment news business is an area over which we have cognizance."

"Well, Mr. President, that is a bit disappointing, but I guess I'll have to find somebody who can write up a legislative proposal."

"It shouldn't be hard, Miss Lopez. Washington's full of people who can do it."

"I suppose that's true, Mr. President," Lopez said. "The people on my staff certainly aren't all that literate. We find that people who read and write well are dangerous as employees. They tend to see things or get ideas and tweet them."

"I see. Well, maybe you can find a good consultant," Obama said.

"True. Thank you for your time, Mr. President. I think we'll leave now. G'bye."

"Goodbye, Miss Lopez. It was a pleasure."

Jennifer Lopez and Ryan Reynolds got out of the car and walked away.

Biden asked, "Mr. President, did you say we have specifically enumerated powers in the Constitution?"

"Yes, I did, Joe, but I only brought it up as a way to

discourage Miss Lopez. We never really pay attention to any Constitutional limits on the Presidency."

"Hmmm," Biden said, "I really ought to read that thing someday."

Chapter Ten

YOUTH IS AS YOUTH DOES

"Politics is the skilled use of blunt objects."

- *Lester B. Pearson*

The Obama entourage arrived at Americorps headquarters in force and pulled into VIP parking. The bumper and rear quarter panel on the presidential SUV was being held together with duct tape.

President Obama and his group got out of the SUV and were greeted by a lineup of Americorps personnel. The group was dressed in a mashup of mismatched polo shirts, casual slacks, and an occasional pair of jeans. One man wore a tool belt. They were standing at attention, sort of.

A heavyset, elderly woman named Helen Smith

introduced herself and welcomed the President and his group.

"Thank you, Helen," Obama said. "Is Mr. Gumpferts here today?"

"Uh, no sir, he isn't," Helen said. "He's on leave, sir. We would have called him in, but he is in South America and we couldn't reach him."

"Interesting. What is he doing there?" Obama asked.

"Well, Mr. President, he is on vacation with his family. He is skiing and playing golf I believe."

"I see. Do you work for him?"

"Oh, no sir. I work for Jane Willsap, the Director and Coordinator for Federal Agency Liaison. She works for him."

"I see. Is she here?" Obama asked.

"Uh, no sir, she is not. She is also on leave."

"I see."

"Yes, sir. She is in Belize," Helen offered.

"Well, Helen," Obama asked, "is anyone here from the top level of Americorps management?"

"Uh, well, no sir. They're pretty much all out in the field or on leave right now."

"I see," Obama said.

"This meeting was on pretty short notice, sir. We're here to help you if we can, though."

Obama looked at the lineup of Americorps personnel and wasn't encouraged.

"Well, can we go inside and have a meeting, Helen?"

"Oh, yes sir. The big conference room is available. We just finished a sexual harassment seminar for our field managers."

"Very good, Helen," Obama said.

The two groups walked into the Americorps headquarters building past some displays of young people building houses and fences and teaching in schools. They were led into a conference room that had about fifteen small folding chairs and a small folding table that would accommodate about six people.

After everyone crowded in and settled down Helen kicked it off.

"Well, sir, what can we do for you?"

"Helen, we're here on a fact finding trip to see how the Stimulus money has helped Americorps deliver better services to its client agencies and to the clinics and school districts you support. According to my tracking sheet we sent about twelve billion in Stimulus money to Americorps to escalate your activities."

"Twelve billion, sir? My goodness, that sounds like a lot. I remember that we recruited about fifty more people this year than last year. I asked Ms. Willsap to ask Mr. Gumpferts if we could bring in any more people, but she said he was reluctant to do that due to downward budget pressure."

"Does anyone else here know anything about how the Stimulus money was used here at Americorps?" Obama asked.

The man with the tool belt raised his hand.

"Yes?" Obama asked.

"Stan Gordon, Mr. President. I'm with maintenance. I think I know how we used the money here at Americorps. We were able to get three new ladders and six cordless drills. Came in real handy."

"I see," Obama said. "Does anyone have anything else?"

Everyone at the table was silent. They looked around at each other and remained quiet for several long seconds. Finally Helen said, "I think that's all we know right now, Mr. President. I'll place calls to our managers to let them know what your primary issues are and try to get them to answer the questions about the Stimulus money."

"Thank you, Helen. I look forward to hearing from

them. Please ask Mr. Gumpferts to call me when he calls in," Obama said. "Ladies and gentlemen, it's been a pleasure meeting you."

The groups shook hands and Obama headed out with his people. They climbed into the SUVs and drove off.

"Well, Mr. President," Biden said, "I think that went well."

"Thanks, Joe. David, let's run an audit on them. I want to make sure that whatever happened to that money doesn't surface with the media."

"Yes, sir. Any specific instructions, Mr. President?"

"Yes. I'd like an accounting of twelve billion dollars minus three ladders and six cordless drills."

Chapter Eleven

SMALL BUSINESS

"The key is to commit crimes so confusing that police feel too stupid to even write a crime report about them."
— *Randy K. Milholland*

"Where to next?" Obama asked.
"Well, sir, the bagel shop is close by," Axelrod said.
"Good, let's head over there."
Two minutes later the dented, rattling presidential SUV caravan pulled up outside the *Senate Bagel and*

Doughnut Shoppe. Signs outside the shop promised good coffee and great doughnuts and bagels. The place looked like it was about to close up. A middle-aged man was sweeping up and telling customers that he would close in about fifteen minutes.

The President and his group got out of the SUV and headed for the store. The man looked up and rolled his eyes skyward.

"We're closing up in ten minutes and I'm out of most of the bagels. I don't have any doughnuts left."

"Sir, I'm President Obama," Obama said holding out his hand to shake hands.

"I'll bet you are," the man said while he continued to sweep.

"No, really. I am."

The man stopped sweeping and looked hard at the President. "Well you sure look like him."

"That's because I am him."

"Hmm. Well, Mr. President," the man said as he wiped his hands off on his apron and held out his hand to shake hands, "I'm Sal."

"Are you the owner?" Obama asked.

"Not technically. I'm married to her."

"Is she here?"

"No. No, she isn't."

"Well, then," Obama said, "can we talk?"

"Sure, sure. Just give me a minute."

The remaining customers were staring by this time. Sal asked them all to pack up and leave because he had to close up early. There was some "Aw, Sal" and "Can't we stay?" kinds of grumbling as they cleared out. Sal locked the door.

"Uh, sorry, sir. Now, what can I do for you?"

"Well, Sal, we're here to see how your business is

doing with the Stimulus money we gave you."

"Stimulus money?"

"Yes. Our tracking sheet shows you received about three and a half million dollars for business expansion. Has it helped?"

"Stimulus money, huh? That's where that damned money came from."

"What money are you talking about, Sal?" Obama asked.

"Well," Sal said, "Martha had an application in for a small business loan for a woman owned business. She was asking for about a hundred thousand to remodel."

"A hundred thousand?"

"Uh, yes sir. But she came in one day a little happier than I'd seen her for a while. She said the loan money came in. She said she got a little more than she asked for and decided to head out to talk to contractors to start a remodel. She said something about our remodeling project being shovel ready as she headed out."

"Well, that sounds promising, Sal," Obama said.

"But that's the last I seen of her."

"When was that?"

"About three months ago, I think," Sal said.

"Where did she go?" Obama asked.

"I'm not sure, but our accountant thinks she's in Vegas or the Bahamas somewhere. He says he seen receipts from those places on our store credit card," Sal said as he stared at the floor and sighed.

"I see. Well, Sal," Obama said hesitatingly, "uh… thank you for your time. I hope your business keeps growing."

"Growing, huh? I hope it starts growing. Need any bagels? We got some plain ones left."

"Uh, sure. David, could you get a dozen for us and the

crew?"

"Yes, sir," Axelrod said. As the group left Axelrod completed a transaction for a mix of the remaining bagels from the shop.

They all piled into the back of the SUV.

"Well, that was weird," Biden said. "I wonder why she went to Vegas and the Bahamas to get contractors to remodel her store."

Obama said, "David, can I get one of those bagels? I'm a little hungry."

Obama took a raisin bagel and passed the bag around. They all bit into the bagels at about the same time and had a similar reaction.

"This bagel is hard as a rock," Obama said.

The group all looked around at each other and at the bagels. They were momentarily at a loss for words when Biden spoke up, "I think it's an ethnic thing, Mr. President. People from some parts of the world really like hard bagels, I'm figuring."

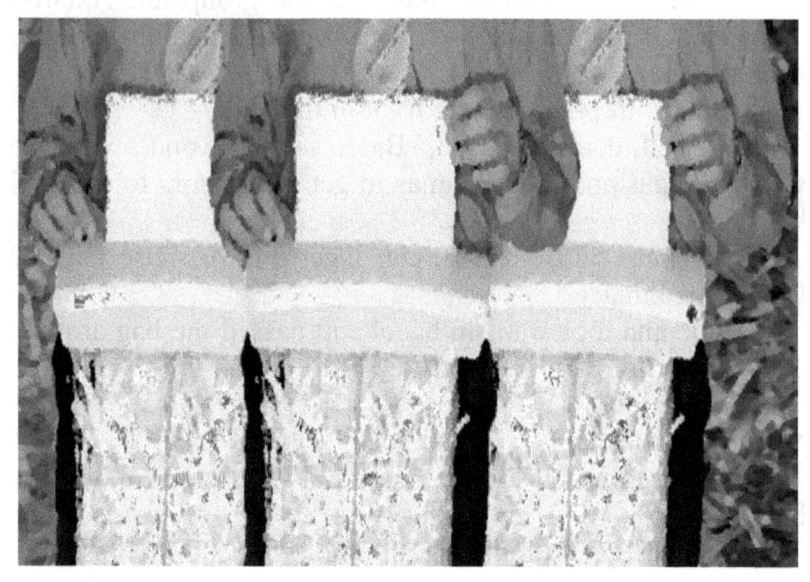

Chapter Twelve

A SHRED OF TRUTH

"Politics is made up largely of irrelevancies."

- *Dalton Camp*

The address of the MAGA offices was in Georgetown. The President's SUV caravan rattled its way across town to get there before the business day was over. The SUV group pulled up to park next to a gray, non-descript office building.

"This is the address, Mr. President," Axelrod said.

There was no sign on the building that indicated any specific organization was located there. Axelrod and Biden walked up to the building entrance with Obama and the Secret Service trailing behind. Biden tested the entrance door and found that it was locked. He put his face up to the glass and shielded his eyes with his hands to look inside. He could see a sleeping guard at a security console.

Biden banged on the door and rattled it. The young guard woke up, looked around to get his bearings, and then squinted over at the door. He got up slowly and walked over to look at the waiting group. The guard shrugged his shoulders and said "It's locked" as he pointed at the door. He made a miming gesture indicating a key in a lock.

"Unlock it!!" Biden yelled.

The guard pulled a walkie-talkie off his belt and talked into it. After a couple of exchanges he came over to the door, pulled out a card key, passed it over an electronic reader, and unlocked the door.

"Thank you, son. I'm Vice President Joe Biden and I'm here with President Obama."

"I thought you guys looked familiar. I'm John, the security guard."

"Why is this building locked up?" Biden asked.

"Well, sir, the building is always locked up. It's all card key entry. We almost never have to let anybody in. Everybody who is supposed to get in gets in with a card key."

"What about visitors?"

"That's a good question, sir. I haven't had that problem before."

"I see," Biden said.

"We're here to see the MAGA offices," Obama said.

"MAGA, huh? Let me see." The guard takes a quick look at the building directory. "Uh, sir, how do you spell MAGA?"

"M-A-G-A."

"Hmm. Here it is. Suite Seven Six Seven."

"Seven sixty seven. Thanks. We're going to head on up there," Obama said.

"Well, sir," the guard said, "you need a card key to work the elevator. You can have mine I guess. You are the President, and all."

"Well, thank you, John," Obama said. "Your trust in me is touching."

"Yes, sir. I would like the card back before you leave, sir. I have to pass it on to the next guard."

"No problem, John. Thanks again," Obama said.

The group got on the elevator and headed up to the seventh floor. After walking around the seventh floor for some time the group approached a plain office door with a small set of numbers mounted on the door indicating '767'. There was no doorbell or card key entry mechanism.

Biden knocked on the door. After several seconds he knocked more loudly. Finally, he pounded on the door.

The door flew open and an angry looking bearded man stood in the door frame. "WHAT??? What do you want?"

Biden stared at the man for a second. He stared back.

"You all look familiar," the man said.

Biden shook his head, looked around, put his hands on his hips, and focused on the man standing in the doorframe. "Well, sir. I'm the Vice President of the United States, Joe Biden. This is the President, Barack Obama."

"Yeah, and I'm the f*#&ing Pope."

"Take another look, smart ass. Who do we look like?"

"I don't know. Donald Trump and Michael Jordan?"

Obama broke in, "Is your manager here?"

"I'm the manager."

"Well, we need to talk to you," Obama said.

"We're kinda busy right now. We were told that some people were coming over and we thought it was Fox and Breitbart's people. We're shredding right now. Lots of shredding."

"That was us," Axelrod said. "We called ahead."

"Oh. It was you," the manager said. "Sorry. We didn't really believe the President would come here. We decided it was some kind of raid so we started shredding. We still got a lot of shredding to do."

"We need to talk to you still, Mr...?"

"Uh, Smith. My name's Smith. Joe Smith."

"Mr. Smith," Obama said, "can we come in and talk?"

"Sure, Mr. President. Right this way."

They follow Joe Smith through the offices to a conference room in the back of the office suite. The group passes more than ten people who are engaged in document stacking and shredding. Piles of paper were stacked up in numerous places awaiting the shredding operation.

"So, Mr. Smith," Biden said, "we're here about the Stimulus money. We want to know how the Stimulus money you received has helped create jobs."

"Stimulus money?" Smith asked. "How much we talkin'?"

"Four billion according to our tracking sheet," Obama said.

"Oh, that money. That money was very helpful. It created a lot of jobs. Community organizers, protesters, sign makers, community organizers, bus drivers, audio and video specialists, community organizers, bloggers, opposition researchers, and community event organizers."

"I was a community organizer once," Obama said.

"So I've heard, Mr. President. Well, we were able to expand our operations significantly. For about six months we grew about a hundred percent."

"How many people is that?"

"Well we're normally at about twenty five people so we grew to about fifty folks. We didn't have any additional room here so a lot of them worked at home."

"You say this lasted six months? Then what happened?" Obama asked.

"Well we ran out of Stimulus money and had to scale back."

"Twenty five people ran through four billion dollars in six months?" Obama asked.

"Personnel costs are a bitch these days," Smith said.

"So what did they accomplish?" Obama asked.

"Well, they organized a lot of events and made a lot of loans."

"You made loans with the money?"

"Well, sir, not exactly," Smith said. "We helped people get loans."

"What did your organization do to help people get loans?" Obama asked.

"We, uh, we helped them produce their paperwork and file the applications for their loans. Then we tracked the loan process. Then we helped distribute the loans."

"Distribute the loans? What does that mean?" Obama asked.

"We passed the loan proceeds on to the recipients."

"So let me understand. The loans passed through your accounting system?" Obama asked.

"Uh, yes sir."

"Why did the loan money come to you first?"

"Well, Mr. President we wanted to be able to track the loan recipients and the distribution process. We wanted to do a better job than we did with our prior loan encouragement efforts."

"I see. So you distributed all of the money so far?" Obama asked.

"We've made all of the distributions, yes, sir."

"All of the money?" Obama pressed.

"Well, uh, except for our processing support fees," Smith said.

"And how much were your organization's fees?" Obama asked.

"The whole thing was on a point system depending on the risk profile of the loan. Some of the low risk loans were assessed fees at about two points. High risk loans ran as high as ten points."

"Points mean a percentage?"

"Sort of. A point is... uh... is about...uh... five percent or so," Smith said.

Obama and his group were momentarily stunned. They looked at each other and back at Joe Smith.

"Any other Stimulus money supported efforts we should know about, Joe?" Obama asked.

"Well, we had training, sir."

"What kind of training?"

"For community organizers, sir."

"Ah," Obama said, "I used to do that kind of training. We used Saul Alinsky's text – *Rules for Radicals*. Great book. Is that what you used?"

"I think we got some curriculum material from Bill Ayers. Same kind of thing though, Mr. President," Smith said.

Obama and the group wrapped up the meeting, said their thanks and goodbyes, and left the offices walking toward the elevator.

"Who has the card key?" Obama asked.

"The card key, sir?" Biden asked.

"For the elevator."

Biden and Axelrod started checking all of their pockets. None of them could remember who had the card key. Biden finally found the card in his shirt pocket after having checked it several times.

"Here it is," Biden said smiling.

While the elevator made its way up to the seventh floor they were all thinking about their visits during the day.

"David, I want to get a team over here to help MAGA out."

"Good idea, Mr. President. What do you want me to tell them to do?" Axelrod asked.

"Tell 'em to pitch in. And they should bring some more shredders."

Chapter Thirteen

MAKE A NEW PLAN, STAN

"Politics is war without bloodshed while war is politics with bloodshed."

- *Mao Tse-Tung*

The rag-tag presidential SUV caravan clinked and rattled its way back to the sanctity of the White House. Obama, Biden, and Axelrod pulled themselves out of the back seat while showing signs of weariness.

"Hey, guys," Obama said, "Michelle went up to New York with the girls to go shopping. Wanna come up for a beer?"

"Sure," Biden said. "My wife went with her."

"Yes, sir. We can talk about where we go from here," Axelrod said.

"We might talk about that a little, David, but I need to let my brain rest. Let's talk while we watch a ball game or something," Obama said.

The group headed upstairs to the presidential living quarters. They settled into a living room area with a big screen television and found a basketball game on an ESPN channel.

Biden, Axelrod, and Obama were into their second beer when they all reacted to a noise. They looked away from the television in the direction of the door to the bedroom.

Their mouths dropped open simultaneously.

"Barack?" The query came from a deep voice that they all heard. A spectral image stood in front of them that appeared to be a semi-transparent semblance of Abraham Lincoln. "Well, Barack? Don't you recognize me?"

"President Lincoln?"

"Yep," Lincoln said.

"Really? C'mon…uh…sir. I'm afraid I don't believe in ghosts."

"I don't believe in paying people for doing nothing, but nobody's been asking my opinion lately," Lincoln said.

"Well, Mr. President," Obama said, "you have to understand our skepticism. We've got a lot of talented friends in Hollywood who could rig up a gag like this with some new imaging technology or something. Somebody could be projecting your image in the room here."

"Ya think?" Lincoln asked. "Sounds amazing. But I'm not a gag, and that's not how I got here."

Obama got up out of his chair. Biden and Axelrod remained coiled up and shaking with fear.

"Do you mind if I... if I touch you?" Obama asked.

"Be my guest," Lincoln answered.

Obama moved forward and cautiously put his hand out. As he approached the image, Lincoln said, "When you put your hand inside you'll feel pretty cold. I just want to warn you."

Obama reached the edge of Lincoln's image, slowly put his hand out, and reached inside. A sudden cold sensation shot through Obama's body. His back straightened involuntarily, and he reflexively pulled his hand back.

"Are you all right, Mr. President?" Axelrod asked.

"I don't know why it feels like that," Lincoln said. "Nobody's been able to explain it to me."

Obama was shivering and rubbing his hands on his arms in an effort to warm up. "That's very cold. I don't understand. Do you guys know who set this up?" Obama asked looking at Biden and Axelrod.

"Nobody set this up, Barack. I'm the real deal. Well, not as real as when I was alive, but it is me. It's not some Hollywood trick, although I must admit I've been very entertained by how creative they are out there."

"C'mon, Spielberg could do this couldn't he?"

"I'm as real as a ghost can be, President Obama," Lincoln said.

"You know, I still don't believe in ghosts," Obama said. He looked back at Biden and Axelrod who were still coiled up on the couch with their eyes wide open.

"I didn't really believe in ghosts either until I came back to visit here every once in a while. The halls were full of them. Still are. There are more ghosts here now than there were in my day," Lincoln said.

"I haven't seen any," Obama protested.

"You haven't been looking," Lincoln said. "You know what made me finally believe in ghosts, President Obama?"

"What would that be, sir?"

"When I became one. I met George and Thomas. Ben shows up from time to time. Jack Kennedy. Madison. Great guys. We've all started a regular poker game. Saturday nights in the basement. The security guards know enough to stay away."

"What do you play for?" Obama asked.

"Well, the big winner spends the night in the Lincoln bedroom. The loser has to eat Ben Franklin's cooking," Lincoln said.

"How come I haven't seen any of you here before?" Obama asked.

"We don't have to appear to anyone unless we want to. I chose to assume this image of myself tonight." At that point Lincoln transformed himself to appear as a solid human being. The change startled Obama, Biden, and Axelrod and they gasped involuntarily.

"Relax, gentlemen. This is the other way we appear to you on occasion. You wouldn't always recognize us. John Adams likes to shave, cut his hair, put on a contemporary suit, and walk through the White House with some papers or reports acting like he belongs here. He's attended some of your larger meetings and sat in the back."

"Really?"

"Yes," Lincoln said. "Franklin comes in wearing coveralls and a toolbelt like he's part of the maintenance crew. He likes to shock himself doing electrical repairs. Says it feels good. Jefferson puts on a set of overalls and flirts with the girls on the cleaning crew."

Obama sat down in a chair. His eyes involuntarily blinked several times.

"I know, I know," Lincoln said. "We called it disbelief in my day. You folks call it cognitive dissonance or something. It takes a while to process this."

"Do you come here often, President Lincoln?" Obama asked.

"Not so much anymore except for the poker games. I tailed off after Clinton got elected. Couldn't stand the guy. He was the master of insincerity in my opinion, and he did terrible things in the Lincoln bedroom. You can understand my disgust."

Biden and Axelrod chuckled a bit at this. Obama glared at them and then turned his attention back to Lincoln. "Sir, why are you appearing to us now?" Obama asked.

"Well, Barack, I drew the low card," Lincoln said. "We decided we needed to talk to you. They sent me as…" Lincoln's sentence tailed off while he thought for a second.

"As what, sir?" Obama asked.

"I guess you could say I'm the Ghost of the United States Past," Lincoln said.

Biden lit up at this statement. "Wow, this is great! It's like that story by Sherlock Holmes, *Great Expectations*," Biden said.

Axelrod said, "Charles Dickens, Mr. Vice President. *A Christmas Carol*."

"Yeah, that's it," Biden said.

Lincoln looked at the three of them and said, "Here we go." Lincoln clapped his hands twice and the three of them suddenly found themselves in a foxhole in a forest during the winter. They were wearing World War II era U.S. Army combat field uniforms and were as bundled up against the cold as they could be. Obama, Biden, and Axelrod started shivering right away.

"Whoa! Where the f*#& are we?" Biden asked.

Before Obama or Axelrod could attempt an answer an artillery barrage started hitting all around them. It splintered trees, pounded the ground, and kicked up large chunks of dirt and wood into their foxhole. The sound was deafening and the concussions were bone rattling as they huddled together hugging the dirt as hard as they could. The barrage let up after a couple of minutes and the group felt relieved that they had not been hit. People were calling for medics on both sides of their position.

"What the hell, Mr. President? We're cold as hell, I'm hungry, and people are trying to kill us. How'd this happen?"

"I don't think I'm the President right now, Joe," Obama said.

At that point Lincoln jumped into the foxhole with them. He was the same tall, strong Lincoln as before, but he was wearing World War II 101st Airborne Division patches and sergeant's stripes on his combat uniform.

"Listen up," Lincoln said.

"Where the f*#& are we?" "What's going on?" and "How'd we get here?" questions were blurted out while the three of them tried to get oriented.

"I'm going to fill you in," Lincoln said. "We have a mission, but…"

"But what?" Obama said.

"Wait a sec. Shut up," Lincoln said.

They all looked up and saw a delegation of World War II German infantrymen walk past their foxhole while surrounded by a guard of armed American soldiers. They were carrying white flags as they walked further into the encampment. As they passed their position Lincoln got up and followed as did Obama, Biden, and Axelrod.

Lincoln looked back at the three of them. "Where are your weapons??? Go get 'em, goddamnit."

Obama, Biden, and Axelrod scrambled back to the foxhole, picked up their Garand M-1 rifles, and ran back to follow Lincoln. He was crouched behind a fallen tree and watching an exchange between the German soldiers and an American soldier who appeared to be the commander of the

U.S. Army troops at their site.

"Who's that?" Obama asked pointing in the direction of the Army commander.

"That's General McAuliffe. Now be quiet. I want to hear what he's saying."

They could see the German army officer had handed a piece of paper to a colonel who handed it to McAuliffe. He read the message carefully, folded up the paper and handed it back to the colonel. "Nuts," they could hear McAuliffe say.

"Nuts, sir?" the American officer asked.

"That's what I said, Colonel, Nuts. N-U-T-S. Nuts," McAuliffe said.

"Yes, sir."

Sergeant Lincoln started chuckling. "That's Tony McAuliffe for you. I've known him since before the war. He's a no nonsense guy. Unfortunately, the Germans aren't going to take too kindly to his response. Let's go."

Sergeant Lincoln, Obama, Biden, and Axelrod headed out and kept on walking till they approached the edge of the forest. Axelrod's head was on a swivel as he kept looking left and right. Biden's helmet kept rattling as he shook from a combination of fear and hypothermia.

"Where are we going, sir?" Biden asked.

"Sir?? Don't call me 'sir', Biden. I'm a sergeant. I work for a living. And strap on that helmet. You're making too much of a racket."

"Uh, okay. Sergeant Lincoln. Where are we going?"

"Everybody listen up," Lincoln said while they were still moving forward through the woods. "We've got a mission. A squad of German spotters has gotten a little too close for comfort and we're going to run 'em off."

Lincoln signaled for the squad to get down on the ground. He started crawling forward and after about ten yards looked back. Obama, Biden, and Axelrod had not moved so he signaled for them to come forward. Biden got up to walk forward.

""Get down you idiot! Crawl forward. You're close to the front! Wanna get your head shot off?"

"Right. No, sir…uh… Sarge." Biden dropped back down to the ground and they all crawled forward behind Sergeant Lincoln.

The squad finally reached the edge of the woods and crawled up behind a fallen tree trunk. Sergeant Lincoln took a pair of binoculars and looked over the log to survey the open field in front of them. "Ah, there they are," Lincoln said. "They're about two hundred yards out."

Just then a mortar round hit too close for comfort. Another round got even closer.

"We've got to move!" Lincoln said. "Over there! Run!" he said pointing to a pile of rocks about twenty five yards to their right.

"Go! Go!" Lincoln yelled. Biden and Axelrod got up and ran as hard as they could. They both fell a couple of times and finally made it to crouch behind the rocks. Small arms fire peppered the ground all around them.

Lincoln got up to run and saw Obama frozen in fear behind the log. "Get up! You'll get hit here. Come on." Lincoln reached down and grabbed Obama by the front of his jacket. He jerked him up to his feet and pushed him to start running. "Run! Run!"

They ran to the position behind the rocks dodging small arms fire all along the way. As Obama hit the ground he said, "Oh, my God. I thought we were going to get killed. Oh, my God."

Sergeant Lincoln started groaning. He was bleeding rapidly through his coat. The bullet hole appeared to be in his chest close to his heart. Obama grabbed him and put his arm around him.

"I'm hit, Corporal Obama," Lincoln said haltingly. "I'm…not going…to make it…You're in charge. You've got to run those guys off…What's your plan?"

"What's the plan, Barack?" Biden asked.

"Do you have a plan, Corporal Obama?" Axelrod asked.

Lincoln's breathing was more labored and he was in terrible pain. "I've…only got…a minute… or two….You've …got to get….a plan… going. You… need… a… plan. You… can't wait… until… the next election," Lincoln gasped. He then appeared to pass away as Biden and Axelrod looked on in horror.

Bullets started to hit all around their position. Biden looked up as the German infantry started to advance on their position.

"We need a plan, Barack," Biden pleaded.

"What's the plan, sir?" Axelrod asked.

At that point, Sergeant Lincoln's body faded away and disappeared.

Chapter Fourteen

SHUT THE FRONT DOOR

"Nothing can so alienate a voter from the political system as backing a winning candidate."

- *Mark B. Cohen*

Suddenly Obama, Biden, and Axelrod found themselves back in the White House. They were all breathing heavily and rubbing their hands in an attempt to warm up.

"Wow," Biden said, "what do you think that meant?"

"I've got no idea," Obama said, "He said I needed to have a plan before the next election. I have a plan. We have good plans. We plan to win the next election."

"Maybe he was referring to some other plan. Maybe a

plan for the economy or national security or something," Axelrod said.

Biden rubbed his face and slapped himself a couple of times. "I tell you what," Biden said, "I'm wiped out. Being out in the cold like that made me tired. I think I'll head home."

"Not so fast, Biden," a familiar voice said. The group looked up to see Ronald Reagan leaning up against the end of a bookcase. He had his legs and arms crossed.

"I need you guys for a bit," Reagan said.

"President Reagan?" Obama asked.

"That's me," Reagan replied.

"But you're not transparent like Lincoln was," Biden said.

"Oh, Lincoln likes that ghost crap. I like the solid look myself," Reagan replied.

"President Reagan," Obama asked, "what can we do for you?"

"I need for you to go with me. I want to show you something. All of you."

"Are you the ghost of U.S. Present?" Axelrod asked.

"Good guess, Axelrod. You're up on your Dickens I'm guessing."

"Lucky guess, Mr. President,"

"I'll say," Reagan said and he clapped his hands twice. Obama, Biden, and Axelrod found themselves in an extremely cold, snowy, desolate landscape standing beside a fracking and oil recovery rig.

"Whoa, Mr. President," Biden said. "I wonder where we are."

"I've got no idea," Obama said, "but we've got to get inside out of this weather or we'll freeze to death."

The three of them climbed the stairs of the fracking platform and saw an observation and control room that overlooked the rig. They climbed up to the outside door of the control room and pulled on the hatch handle to open it.

"Get the hell in here fast!" a man yelled. The three of them scrambled inside and closed the door. "This room drops ten degrees every time that door opens. Who are you guys?"

"Uh, sir, we were dropped off here. Assumed we were supposed to report in," Obama said.

"Sir? Don't call me sir," the man said. He flipped off the hood of his fur lined coat and revealed that he was Ronald Reagan. "I'm the shift super. Call me Ron."

"Sure, Ron," Obama said. "I'm Barack. This is Joe and David."

"Barack? What the hell kind of name is that? You better get a handle or a nickname before you go to the bar, fella. The riggers there'll run you out on your ass."

"What's wrong with Barack?" Obama asked.

"I'm gonna call you Rock. You better hope it sticks. I'm doing you a favor."

"Hmmm," Obama said. "Where are we, Ron?"

"Williston, North Dakota. Dead of winter. And I mean dead."

"Williston, North Dakota? Why are we here?!?"

"Because this is where the oil is. Where the oil is, is where the jobs are. Any more questions?"

"No," they all say meekly.

Reagan said, "All right guys let's get to work. Joe and David, you guys go in the next room there and coil up the rope, straighten out that rat's nest of chains, stack the boxes, and get that equipment room cleaned out and organized."

"Will do, Ron," Joe said.

"Rock, I need you to watch the station here for a minute. I've got to go outside and do visual checks on some things and make a head call. If this pressure gauge here goes into the red an alarm will go off and I need you to pull this valve release handle to the left to relieve the pressure. Got it?"

"Uh, yeah, Ron, I'll do it."

"Gauge in the red, alarm, valve handle to the left. You can remember that, right?"

"I've got it."

"Remember – dead of winter. Temp is six below with a wind chill down to thirty eight below. Don't go outside unless you're suited up properly. Just remember -- we're pumping oil for our customers – the American people. Ain't life grand?"

Ron Reagan zipped up his coat, put on his gloves, put on his ski mask, pulled up his goggles, opened the door, and headed out on the platform. The blast of cold air had them all shivering right away.

"This one is really weird, Rock," Biden said.

"I'll say," Obama said. "You guys get started on the equipment room. When Ron comes back I'll come in and help."

After about five minutes Obama noticed the pressure on the gauge face rising quickly. When the gauge needle touched the red zone sirens, alarms, and lights started to go off. The racket was deafening as Obama reached for the valve handle. Biden and Axelrod rushed back into the control room.

Obama pulled hard on the handle and it wouldn't budge. "Damn thing won't move! Help me out!"

All three of them reached out to grab the handle and attempted to coax it to move. The pressure reading on the gauge continued to climb. The three of them couldn't get the handle to budge. As they were pulling on it Reagan ran into the control room.

"Get out of the way!" he yelled.

Obama, Biden, and Axelrod let go and Ron grabbed

the handle. He put his foot up on the gauge panel for leverage and pulled hard. The valve handle moved slowly to the left and finally hit the position that opened the relief valve.

"Get me some duct tape! It's back in the equipment room!" Reagan yelled as he worked to chain the valve handle in place.

Biden came out with a big roll of silver duct tape. Reagan grabbed it out of his hands and ran outside onto the platform deck. He quickly and expertly wrapped a pipe that was oozing oil from one of the threaded corner fittings. Within two minutes Reagan was done and back in the control room.

The emergency adrenaline was still coursing through their systems as they stared at each other. "You're pretty good with the duct tape, Ron."

"You know we won the World War II with this stuff."

"Were you in World War II?"

"Not really, but I helped make a training film about using duct tape to do a lot of common repairs on Army equipment. Got pretty good with it," Reagan said.

"How'd you get so strong?" Obama asked.

"Nancy made me start lifting weights after I got shot at once. She wanted me to be able to flex my biceps."

They were all quiet for a couple of seconds. Biden finally spoke up, "Why are we out here pumping this greasy oil? We've been trying to convert everything to solar and wind energy."

"No you haven't," Ron said. "You've been throwing money at your buddies and promoting a technology that isn't cost effective without government subsidy. We'll get there eventually, but in the meantime we still need oil and we need to get it from sources that aren't belligerent, hateful, and stupid like most of the Middle Easterners seem to be."

"But the environmentalists say it's bad to drill for oil"

Biden said.

"How is it bad?" Ron asked, "Environmentalists don't seem to care much if we drill for oil in other parts of the world. Sometimes I think they're in the pockets of the Middle East Imams, princes, and oil barons. They do their work for them with American lawyers and legislators."

"We've got oil and natural gas here," Reagan added. "We need to develop our own energy sources as part of our economic recovery and for our national security. It makes us weak to depend on countries that hate us," Ron said.

"But it's a finite resource and we're getting along better with the Middle East," Obama said.

"Oh, for cripe's sake. Those bastards want to kill you and everybody else in the United States. Grow up," Reagan said.

"That's why we've got to do solar," Biden said.

"Aw, shut up, Joe," Reagan said. "All you guys are doing is throwing money at your political cronies. I've got no problem with solar and other energy technologies as long as they work and they're effective in the marketplace. Right now, they don't deliver without government subsidies and you know it."

Ronald Reagan began to turn transparent and fade away. As he faded he repeated, "Do the right thing, Rock. Do the right thing," several times.

After Reagan finally disappeared, Obama, Biden, and Axelrod stared at each other. Suddenly alarms went off all over the control center. Oil started to spray from several pipes on the platform. One of the pipes caught fire and a fast growing, intense inferno started up and spread rapidly.

"Run!!" Obama yelled.

The group cleared the platform and managed to run about fifty yards before a large explosion knocked them all down.

Chapter Fifteen

SOUP'S ON

"Look, John's last-minute economic plan does nothing to tackle the number-one job facing the middle class, and it happens to be, as Barack says, a three-letter word: jobs. J-O-B-S, jobs."

- *Joe Biden*

Obama, Biden, and Axelrod found themselves back in the White House living quarters.
"Geeze oh Pete," Biden said. "This has been one helluva night. What the heck is going on?"

"I'm not sure," Obama said. "I hope that's the last of them, though. I don't think I could take another ghost sighting."

"Ghosts!?!" a voice shouted from behind the bar. "You're calling us ghosts?!?"

Obama's group swung around to look in the direction the voice had come from. They saw three men standing behind the bar. Each had a pewter mug in hand and they were wearing Revolutionary War era clothing. They looked remarkably like George Washington, Thomas Jefferson, and Ben Franklin.

"Who are you?" Obama asked.

"I think I know who they are. President Washington, President Jefferson, and Ben Franklin, Mr. President," Axelrod said.

"We're some of the guys who helped frame this country," Washington said. "It's had its bumps with race relations and other major issues, but it's still the best country in the world. Don't you feel that way, Barack?"

"I ...uh... I do feel that way, Mr. President," Obama said.

"Then why are you trying to wreck it?" Franklin asked.

"I'm not trying to wreck anything," Obama protested.

"Yeah?" Jefferson asked. "What's this Obamacare thing? You told everybody it would be universal. You're exempting more and more organizations every day. If it's good for everybody it should include everybody, shouldn't it?"

"Well, some organizations have their own health care in place," Obama said.

"A lot of organizations do. How are you picking the winners and losers in this?" Washington asked.

"They apply for a... uh... a waiver," Obama said

somewhat meekly.

"How? How do they apply?" Franklin asked. "Where's the application form? What are the criteria? Who decides? Who's been approved and who's been denied and for what reason? Trust me, Barack, we've looked all over the web for this and can't find a damned thing. I run a printing firm. Can I get a waiver?"

"Whoa, Ben, hang on," Obama said. "One question at a time."

"You know," Jefferson said, "we all tried to read that damned bill you signed. Have you read it? Do you know what it all means or how the damned lawyers will interpret it?"

"Look guys, it's complicated," Obama said.

"Ya think?" Washington said. "I've had enough. Let's go."

"Wait! Are you guys the ghosts of the future U.S.A.?" Obama asked.

"Something like that," Washington said as he looked at his friends and nodded.

Washington, Jefferson, and Franklin clapped their hands loudly. Within a split second, Obama, Axelrod, and Biden were inside a large, gray, concrete building wearing kitchen aprons. They each had a big long-handled soup ladle in their hands that was dipped in a big soup pot. Their soup pots were being heated by gas burners on a restaurant sized stove.

"Is that soup ready, Barack?" Franklin shouted.

Obama looked in his direction and saw Ben Franklin with his hair pulled back in a ponytail, wearing a hairnet, and sporting a large, dirty apron. As he looked around he saw a long line of people holding bowls and spoons. They all seemed to wear the same expression as if they had lost all hope. The people were standing patiently in line, but none of them talked.

"Obama!! Is it ready?! Joe!! David!! Is your soup ready?" Franklin asked.

Obama turned to his soup pot and stirred it again. It was steaming and the few vegetables in the soup were softened to the point he thought it was ready.

"I think we're okay here," Obama said.

"You think we're okay??!!" Franklin asked. "Is it boiling? Did you get a temp reading?"

"Uh, no, sir," Obama mumbled.

Washington came over with a large cooking thermometer and handed it to him. "One hundred sixty degrees, minimum. Check it!"

Jefferson was at the serving line explaining the delays to people, "We're just a little backed up folks. We're working it. Give us time." The crowd seemed to groan in unison.

"I'm at one sixty five!" Obama yelled.

Franklin came over in a flash, pulled Obama's pot off the burner and put it in a spot on the serving line. He turned back to Obama. "Get started on the next one there!!"

The cycle repeated several times. Obama, Axelrod, and Biden worked their soup pots until they boiled or at least hit one hundred sixty degrees. They shared the cooking thermometer frequently and kept their efforts moving. After the meal had been completely served Franklin came by.

"All right," Franklin said, "ten minutes, then come back here and start cleaning up these pots for dinner."

Obama, Biden, and Axelrod went looking for a place to sit down. They walked into the hall where everyone was seated at large, long tables with benches on each side. There was very little conversation. A few babies were crying.

"What the hell happened here?" Obama asked in a whisper.

"I don't know, sir," Axelrod said. "We could just be

working in some urban soup kitchen somewhere."

"Seems awfully large," Biden said as he looked around at hundreds of people.

Thomas Jefferson walked over to sit with them. "Five minutes, guys," Jefferson said.

"What happened here, President Jefferson?" Obama asked.

"Call me Tom while we're here. But to answer your question, you name it. You're in D.C. right now, by the way. This was the old Homeland Security headquarters building. HLS was shut down after the fighting became pretty widespread in the U.S."

"Fighting here? Who?" Obama asked.

"It would probably be easier to list who wasn't fighting. Drug cartels invaded the south. Some Chinese army divisions landed in the West and in Alaska. Al Qaeda and the Iranians came up through Mexico in an alliance with the cartels. Cubans invaded Florida. More Middle Eastern countries threw in and a couple of South American countries joined in the fight. A lot of the fighting is over foraging. Foraging for food, fuel, vehicles, weapons, and ammunition."

"What started it all?" Obama asked.

"Good question," Jefferson said. "First, I guess it started with the final financial collapse of Europe which led to major financial upheavals in the United States. Even China was having a tough time. Countries were using their military to grab for natural resources. Food started getting scarce. Petroleum was hard to get because suppliers stopped drilling a pumping in some key areas. They couldn't get paid and the work was too dangerous. Wars erupted in about thirty different global border regions."

Ben Franklin and George Washington came by. "You guys about ready to go back to work?" Washington asked.

"Yes, sir," Biden said.

"I have a question first, George," Obama said. "Who is providing this food for these people?"

"Well, we are for the moment," Washington said. "We're now part of the new E.U.S.A. – the Eastern United States of America. We tried to keep it all together, but the West and the Central United States wanted to break off. Our country ends at the Mississippi more or less. The C.U.S.A. starts there. The W.U.S.A. starts at the Rockies somewhere."

"Are we fighting each other?" Axelrod asked.

"Some. I think it would be more intense if we weren't both distracted by external enemies. The West has their problems with Mexico and western Canada as well as anybody who can beach a landing force and defend a position on the west coast."

"Here in the east we have problems with Europeans who want to be here along with Cubans, people from the Caribbean, Muslims coming in through Europe and up through Mexico, and people pouring in through Canada. We may lose Florida and South Carolina fairly soon. Georgia's in jeopardy. There's a lot of sharp fighting in New York and New Jersey. We're not sure about Maine and New Hampshire."

"If we're so screwed up why are they all coming here?" Obama asked.

"It's the wild west show, Barack," Washington said. "They're coming from places that are worse in a lot of ways. Our country still represents opportunity. As a matter of fact, now that the country has broken up and become somewhat destabilized people are seeing a lot of opportunity. Black markets, land grabs, guns, drugs, oil from our producing wells in Texas and North Dakota. The offshore rigs have been overrun, by the way. Russians on the East Coast. China on the west. South America in the Gulf."

"Holy crap, what happened to our military?" Obama

asked.

"After you'd been president for a while there wasn't much left of it. We were down to two active carrier groups with two carriers in reserve, a couple of airwings, and about ten army divisions. They were spread too thin to cover all the threats. There was no money to expand and no willingness in Congress to borrow more. Nobody would buy the bonds anyway. The military ended up leading much of the rebellion that split the country."

"The supreme court?" asked Biden.

"They were executed," Washington said.

"Executed?!?" Obama asked. "When??!"

"The last one was rounded up and shot about a week ago."

"What about the administration??" Obama asked.

"Still looking for a lot of them," Washington said.

At that point a large number of military personnel wearing Kevlar armored vests and carrying assault rifles entered the building. All conversations stopped as the hall became silent. The sounds of people eating stopped. The military unit began walking through the crowd and looking closely at people. Finally they stopped in front of Obama, Biden, and Axelrod.

"You three get up and come with me," an officer told them.

"Where are we going?" Obama asked.

"GET UP!! START MARCHING!!!" the officer yelled.

Obama, Biden, and Axelrod stood up and started walking between two squads of soldiers. They marched out of the building and down the street. They entered a large amphitheater like structure and were marched into the center of an arena that was surrounded by several concentric rows of temporary bleachers.

When they reached the middle of the arena, floodlights hit them from all angles. They couldn't see anyone in the bleachers or see the control booth area positioned behind one section of the bleachers.

A squad marched out into the arena to meet them. "Former President Obama, I take it?" the man leading the squad asked them.

Obama thought the man looked and sounded familiar. "Bill O'Reilly? Are you Bill O'Reilly?" Obama asked.

"I'm Colonel O'Reilly now, Mr. Obama," O'Reilly said.

"I'm President Obama to you," Obama said.

"Not since you abdicated about three months ago. You've been in hiding and we just located you and your entourage. We found a few others and we'll bring them out here too."

"Out here for what?" Obama said.

"For trial. For treason, incompetence, ineffective leadership, and failing to maintain the national security. There are about seven hundred and fifty six charges."

"We want lawyers!" Obama said.

"We have new laws in E.U.S.A., Mr. Obama. Lawyers aren't allowed except in rare circumstances. There aren't many left anyway. We executed a lot of them. Seeing as how you were a lawyer, you are specifically forbidden from being represented by a lawyer. This is a military tribunal anyway. You have to represent yourself," Colonel O'Reilly explained.

"Well, I protest! Who is the authority in this court?" Obama asked.

"I am!!" a voice boomed at high volume through speakers all around the arena.

"Who are you?" Obama asked.

"I am General Rush Limbaugh, Commanding

General of the East U.S.A. armed forces, and I am in charge of these proceedings!"

"This is some kind of joke. Rush Limbaugh? General Rush Limbaugh? You've got to be kidding," Obama said.

"This whole thing might be a joke if anyone were actually laughing," Limbaugh boomed. *"But that hasn't happened since you got elected. In your case, I don't think this is a joke at all."*

"What are we being charged with?"

"I believe Colonel O'Reilly read the list to you," Limbaugh said.

"Those weren't formal charges! That was just a list of opinions off the top of his head! I deserve to see the charges! I want to see the evidence!" Obama demanded.

"Those were the charges and you are the evidence," Limbaugh said. *"Your four plus years in office, which has cost us our country, is the evidence. Your incompetence is the evidence. Your lack of experience and your associations with socialists, communists, and community organizers is the evidence."*

"That's it??? No trial! No evidence! No defense?" Obama protested.

"Defense?? No one here believes there could possibly be any defense for what you've done," Limbaugh said. *"Let me guess. You were going to use the 'Plausible Deniability' defense, weren't you? Or maybe you were going to use the 'Modified Limited Hangout' defense. That's a good one. You'd have to find a scapegoat. Who would that be? Holder? Panetta? Your whole cabinet?"*

Limbaugh continued at full volume through the PA system, *"There's always the tactic of blaming the Bush administration for leaving too many 'unknown unknowns' lying around. None of that will work. Your case has been decided. The sentence, death by firing squad by my order, will be carried out in five minutes."*

Obama, Biden, and Axelrod looked at Colonel O'Reilly who was standing near them.

"Bill, you gotta talk to this guy. This is crazy! We didn't do anything!" Obama said.

"It is a little harsh, I must admit, but there's nothing I can do," O'Reilly said. "What's done is done."

"Harsh?? It's barbaric! A firing squad??? Who does that??" Obama protested. Biden started blubbering and crying. Axelrod stood wide eyed, shaking his head and trembling.

"Oh, Mr. Obama, relax," O'Reilly said. "This is one of the most humane firing squads possible. We'll sedate you and sit you down and then three hundred participants will file into the arena bleachers. Half of them will be firing blanks…or… wait a minute. Is it that half the rounds fired are blanks? Whatever. None of them will know which one of them actually killed you."

"Three hundred people??? Are you insane??!!" Obama said.

"No it's pretty much the opposite of insane actually. We've studied this quite a bit and with that number of people in the firing squad nobody will actually feel as though they delivered the fatal shot. Their feelings are important to us. Everybody is quite relieved. Besides, we will put up paper targets in front of you. They won't even see you."

"This is a circular arena, O'Reilly!!! Isn't that what you call a circular firing squad!?!?!" Obama yelled.

"Well, sort of. But they're all up in the bleachers shooting in a downward direction. They don't hit each other very often. Don't' worry," O'Reilly said.

"Don't worry!!??!! You're telling me 'Don't worry'!?!? You're about to shoot all of us and I'm not supposed to worry???" Obama pleaded.

"Okay. Worry then if it makes you feel better," O'Reilly said. "We've got to get this done. After your group we've got a bunch of union bosses to take care of. NEA, SEIU, AFL-CIO, UAW...all the good ones." O'Reilly then turned his back on Obama and walked away to talk to one of his people.

Soldiers came into the arena with chairs and stanchions with paper targets mounted on them. They marched some additional people into the arena and tied them all to the chairs along with Obama, Biden, and Axelrod. Target stanchions with large bright red, white, and blue target circles printed on paper were placed in front of each chair.

"Wait, O'Reilly," Obama said. "Please come back here. I need to ask you something."

"Hurry up, Mr. Obama. We don't have much time," O'Reilly said.

"Can you get a message to Michelle and the kids?" Obama asked.

"Probably not. They were picked up in a different country according to one report we got," O'Reilly said.

"Another country? Where?"

"Central U.S.A. We don't have great relations with that country. It would be hard to get them to cooperate. My understanding is that the people in the Central U.S.A. are starving. Food's scarce and being controlled by a few former Democrats in what used to be Chicago. When Michelle was told about the problem she told them it would do them good to lose a little weight. She added that they should eat more vegetables," O'Reilly said.

"Then what happened?" Obama asked.

"Well, the reports are a little sketchy, but the girls were led off to live on a farm in Illinois somewhere. Michelle was tried and executed. At least, I think there was a trial. At any rate, the girls are in good hands. They each have a horse now."

"Oh my God," Obama said. "I can't believe this. Listen, Colonel, this is absolutely ludicrous. You and Limbaugh have had it out for me from day one. What the two of you are doing is illegal and you know it. You've got to stop it."

"Well, Mr. Obama, I don't think it is illegal," O'Reilly said. "I remember when you tried to make what we do illegal. You wanted to demand equal time from our radio network for left leaners to do television and radio no matter how incompetent they were at it. Apparently NPR and that lousy Air America wasn't enough. The problem, as I'm sure you know, is that lefties don't know how to entertain without a script. All they could do is rant and try to express their anger at everything. What's ironic about all of this is many of the people who tried it were actually entertainers – comedians or comedic actors. I guess life's really tough without a script or a laugh track. What you and the rest of the left simply don't get is that one of the reasons people listen to us is that Limbaugh and I are truly nice guys. I'm sorry you never saw it that way."

"You can't be serious. You and Limbaugh have never been nice guys," Biden said through his blubbering.

"Speaking for myself specifically, you've got to understand that I have not had it out for you or your administration at all and what you're saying about me is totally unfair. I am an independent as you should know – not a Democrat or a Republican. I told people that repeatedly everyday on my show. I was fair and balanced about you. My fair and balanced assessment of you as President of the United States is that you were the worst president we've ever had…by a country mile. Limbaugh is another story. He was jumping on you from day one. I gave you a whole two weeks."

95

"Oh, come on. Bush left us a total mess," Obama said.

"Now, there you go again. I'm definitely not listening to any more crap about the Bush problems you inherited. You had plenty of time to fix them. You just didn't know how. You were incompetent. That's all there is to it. Besides," O'Reilly said, "I couldn't stop Limbaugh anyway. He outranks me. He's a general. My job is just to carry out his orders."

"Good morning, ladies and gentlemen. I'm coming to you as I always do from behind the golden microphone at the EIB network," Limbaugh's voice boomed over the PA system. *"We've got a great show for you today. We'll get right to the highlight of the whole thing shortly after a word from our sponsor – TailGunner Gun Oil. One application is all you need for days of safe, reliable gun operations."*

"I must warn the listening audience that what you will hear in the next few minutes may not be appropriate for younger listeners or those of you with any kind of physical frailty or heart problems. In just two minutes we will be eliminating the last known elements of the horribly incompetent Obama administration. As a matter of fact, we captured Mr. Obama himself just this morning and he will be joining in the festivities as one of the condemned. He is perhaps the most notable among this particular group of convicted felons who are all guilty of capital offenses. I'm sure that if Mr. Obama could he would tell you how important and accomplished he is at any rate. After all he is a Nobel Peace Prize winner. He got it his first year in office before he'd done anything."

The personnel in the arena with Colonel O'Reilly approached the people who were tied to the chairs and put blindfolds on them. While they were being blindfolded the condemned people could hear the shuffling and rattling of many additional armed people as they filed into the arena bleachers.

At this point, Colonel O'Reilly said a few last words to the condemned. "I'm sorry it has come to this ladies and gentlemen. We all had hopes for a grand future until Mr. Obama was elected. But all of this suffering will be over for you soon. The rest of us will have the burden of having to trudge on somehow."

O'Reilly chuckled a bit at his last remark and then continued, "Just so you know, we have three hundred firing squad participants who will be firing multiple semi-automatic three round bursts – all down into the arena in your direction. You don't have a chance, but take comfort in the fact that it will all be over in seconds. May God be with you."

"Don't we get any last words??!!" Obama screamed.

"You've talked enough already, Mr. Obama. Besides, we have your teleprompter," O'Reilly said.

Biden started to cry more loudly than anyone else. He was moaning and groaning at the top of his lungs. Axelrod's head was down as he sat quietly awaiting his fate. Obama was struggling to get free of the duct tape that bound him to his chair.

"We have to get this in between commercial breaks," Limbaugh's voice boomed again. ***"Is the firing squad ready?"***

All of the uniformed personnel in the stands shouted, "Yes, sir!" in unison.

"Well then, let's get on with it. Attteennnnhut!" Limbaugh shouted as the sound of three hundred assault rifles and six hundred feet were snapped to attention. ***"Ready arms!"*** The condemned group could hear rifles being brought up to the shoulders of the firing squad. Biden kept crying. Axelrod began to breathe deeply.

Obama yelled, "Iiiiii caaaaan't beeelieeeve this

shhhhhiiiiittt!"
"Aim!.. Fire!!!"
The sounds of multiple volleys of massive, simultaneous small arms fire startled Obama, Biden, and Axelrod. The three of them were each surprised that they could hear anything.

Chapter Sixteen

LISTENING AND LEARNING

"You don't lead by hitting people over the head. That's assault, not leadership."

- *Dwight D. Eisenhower*

Obama, Biden, and Axelrod found themselves back in the White House living quarters. They heard the sounds of a basketball game on television and slowly opened their eyes to look around. Obama noticed that Biden and Axelrod were sitting on their hands as if they were tied down. He soon noticed that he was sitting on his hands also. Obama slowly pulled his hands out and rubbed them. Biden and Axelrod followed suit. Biden rubbed the tears from his eyes and face. Axelrod rubbed his head trying to clear his thinking.

"What happened to us tonight?" Obama asked.

"We were shot twice and blown up," Biden said while trying to stop sobbing.

"I think they tried to give us some kind of message," Axelrod said.

"I think that's true, but I wonder what the message really was," Obama said. "We all had the same experiences, didn't we? You guys saw Lincoln, Reagan, Washington, Jefferson, and Franklin?"

"Yeah," Biden said, "and O'Reilly and Limbaugh."

"What do you make of it, though?" Obama asked.

Axelrod said, "I'm really not sure, Mr. President. Maybe they were telling us that we have to work harder. Lead better. Try to pull the country together."

"I think you're right, David," Obama said. "We do have to try harder. We need to double down on our efforts. That's a good interpretation. I think I know what we have to do."

Obama looked at Biden and Axelrod. They were staring back at President Obama in anticipation of his remarks. Obama cleared his throat and said, "Here's what we're going to do. We're going to start by expanding government health care even more and making the rich pay a lot more of their fair share. We've gotta make that happen."

"That's it. That's right," Biden said while continuing to wipe the tears from his eyes.

"We need to protect the environment and cut back on oil drilling, fracking, refining, and shipping," Obama said.

"That's right, Mr. President," Axelrod said.

"We need to make more solar panels," Obama said, "or sell the ones we've made already."

"That's right," Biden and Axelrod said simultaneously.

"And we need to build and repair more roads and bridges…and bridges and roads and stuff," Biden said.

"We need to control businesses so that the unions can provide better benefits to their workers," Obama continued.

"Protect the unions. That's right," Biden said.

"And we need to ensure that our friendships around the world are strengthened so that we can cut back on unnecessary expenses for national defense," Obama concluded.

Biden and Axelrod shook their heads up and down in agreement.

Obama said, "Let's call a cabinet meeting for tomorrow morning. We need to get started."

Washington, Jefferson, Franklin, Lincoln, and Reagan watched the President and his cohorts on a giant screen HD television in a heavenly man cave. They were gathered around a pool table at a bar. The five of them were drinking brandy and smoking cigars as they listened in on the conversation. They watched Biden and Axelrod as they continued to express a sickeningly obsequious level of approval for Obama's final interpretation of the messages they received that night.

"Well, do you think they got the message, Tom?" Washington asked.

"Hell no, George, they're not even close," Jefferson said.

"They're further off the mark than they were before we visited," Franklin said. "This appears to be worse than we could have possibly imagined."

"Ronnie, you're the youngest," Lincoln said, "Rack 'em up."

"Will do, Abe," Reagan said. "Is somebody sitting this one out?"

"I think I'll just cheer you presidents on from my

barstool here," Franklin said. "Besides, I want to listen to more of this. I've always found ignorance and bad judgment to be wildly entertaining."

"Well, Ben," Lincoln said, "I've had all the entertainment from those guys I can stand."

"Let us know if they bump their heads and come up with something that might actually make sense," Washington said.

"Will do, George," Franklin said. "Kick some butt over there."

And so it ends...

Soon, hopefully.

Author's Note

My long-suffering lovely wife will tell you. She'll tell you about all the hours I lost yelling at the television when Clinton was President. I really thought that his immaturity, depravity, and dishonesty were the lowest possible benchmark for presidential conduct. Then the Obama administration came along.

A lot of reasonable people will say, "But you're not acknowledging the good things they've done." That's true. I honestly don't know of any good things they've done.

I take that back. They've done an amazing job of revising the history of the Bush administration. They have set records for extending blame for our economic condition well beyond the six month period that they have any right to legitimately claim.

They've also done astounding work accelerating the accumulation of debt and have somehow blamed that on Bush too. And with a couple of lucky exceptions, they've been halfhearted and less than courageous in combating terror. Recently they've announced the gutting of our future military structure to a point that should concern everyone.

Meanwhile the Obama administration has relegated the federal government's number one responsibility, national security, to background status while thrusting fiscally unsound social policies like national healthcare and climate protection legislation to the forefront.

The Justice Department can't track massive numbers of weapons it lost in some kind of indecipherable and unexplainable gun and drug trafficking law enforcement operation. Homeland Security can't figure out what a real terrorist looks like or why we should build a fence at the border. The civilian leadership in the Department of Defense gets distracted by experiments in social policy engineering and is incapable of making the case to build and maintain our best possible military capability.

You can see it pretty much everywhere. We're being targeted economically, politically, and militarily by the major and minor powers of the planet. We currently have an administration that simply isn't competitive and apparently doesn't think anyone out there is really a threat to us. While Obama keeps asking, "Can't we all just get along?" the administration is losing leadership status and global standing on an hourly basis.

Certain phrases kept popping up in discussions with *thoughtful* people (people who voted for Obama and won't admit yet that they made a mistake or that they've given up on the guy). Statements are repeated like "Well, they might be a little out of synch on occasion", or "the country's greatest priority is to provide everyone with health care to lower the costs of health care", or "we've got to keep the unions strong to keep our industrial base."

My friends and I more often hear (or use) sentences and phrases like "one taco short of a combo plate", or "not the brightest set of bulbs in the pack", or "with leadership like this we'd better check the food, guns, and ammunition", or most often a simple "WTF?"

So, I had to vent. I had to express myself about what I think is wrong. My spouse accused me of sitting around complaining and not doing anything about it. Well, this book is me doing something about it.

I hope that my stab at an extended satirical treatment of the adventures of this administration entertains some people and possibly even enlightens a few. I also hope anyone who reads this may even be motivated to get involved and help out. If you truly believe, like I do, that almost anybody (Pee Wee Herman, for example) would be a better

President than Barack Obama then jump in and make sure it happens. We need to get our country back on the right track economically, and we definitely need a stronger national security posture.

It's important to reiterate that this book is not fact. It's fiction. One other thing is important to reiterate...

I mean every word of it.

- Austin Speed

www.ingramcontent.com/pod-product-compliance
Lightning Source LLC
Chambersburg PA
CBHW071305040426
42444CB00009B/1870